My wife, Deborah, beautiful brown eyes flashing,
informs me that if after 24 years of washing my socks,
I don't dedicate this book to her, I am
"dead meat."

That settles that!

Contents

Introduction

This book is my wife Deborah's idea. Prompted by the arrival of two wonderful grandchildren, Samantha, who as I write this, closes in on the grand old age of three, and Peyton, who will soon be two. "You have so many wonderful stories," says Deborah, "our children delighted in them, so will our grandchildren. They will want to know their grandfather's story. It is, after all, part of their heritage."

I really didn't intend it, but the story of one grandfather became the story of a family, a country, an industry, a city, and more than anything else, it became a story of a time and a way of life that exists only in the memories of fewer of us every day.

I am certain some members of the Green family will recall certain events differently than I. Willard claims it was he who scooted up that old elm tree to kidnap the crows. I've always told him his faulty memory is the consequence of too many ketchup sandwiches. Besides which, there is an old rule that I just made up: the guy who writes the book gets to tell the story his way!

Several readers have noted that, given the way my story starts, I seem to have had a life remarkably devoid of troubled times. This, of course, is not true. It's just that life is far too great an adventure, far too much fun, to spend much effort or ink rooting around in the bad times.

Defeats, heartbreak, sorrow? Oh ya, I know all about that.

Who doesn't? But to tell the truth, I've had a wonderful life. Enjoyed almost every moment, and you know what? I plan to enjoy it even more as my grandchildren grow up.

I can't wait until one of them says, "Tell us the pork chop story, Grandpa." At which point I'll suggest that in the interests of helping to support their grandfather in his dotage, they get their parents to buy one of my books!

Part I

The Beginning and the End

The crows sense something is wrong. How else can you explain their strange, hovering silence as they follow us to the edge of town? Ordinarily, they would caw their silly heads off. You know how noisy crows can be. Every once in a while they swoop down as though trying to catch a glimpse of us lying on the car floor. Polly and Charlie are their names. "Black as the inside of a black cat with its tail tied down," my father says. "As black as sin," is how Grandma Green describes them.

We had no way of knowing it at the time, but my sister and I would never see Polly and Charlie again. I wish I could at least have said goodbye to them and to those others I loved so much.

I'm a bit hesitant to tell my grandchildren how we got the crows because their mothers would tear a strip off my hide if any of them ever tried this kind of a stunt. This is the story of my life, though, and I have to be honest, don't I? So I'm going to insert a little disclaimer here for grandchildren of all ages: *Do not, I repeat do not, attempt any of the things I did as a boy!* Well, maybe it's okay to try some of the things, but that does not include climbing dead trees in search of baby crows.

Because that's how we get Polly and Charlie. Way up near the top of an old dead elm tree, stripped of bark and bare as a new-born's bottom, is a huge pile of twigs and other pretty repulsive stuff into which mom crow has deposited several eggs. They hatch, as nature intended, into four young crows, whose raucous demands for food and more food can be heard for miles. Crows are very smart birds that build their nests atop tall trees where only the most foolish of little boys dare climb.

Willard and Orlo are older and obviously smarter than I am, so they stay planted on solid ground, freely offering uncle instructions and warnings as I clamber aloft. Four pairs of midnight eyes anxiously watching the foolhardy action below, peer over the edge of their ramshackle home. The warnings are certainly necessary as both mother and father crow begin dive-bombing me, loudly screeching, I presume, horrible crow threats. Knowing what I do now about kidnapping, you can hardly blame them!

Now, you've got to understand that while I am growing up on that rocky little farm clinging to the edge of the village of Arthur, Ontario, all boys know that the only thing worse than drinking milk after eating chokecherries (which causes instant death, so horrible even the medical journals can't bring themselves to discuss it) is an angry crow going for your eyes. The fact that despite believing both eyes are about to be plucked from my head, I bravely continue my ascent, is proof that soldiers really do fight and die, not for king, queen or country, but rather for the esteem of their peers. What is losing your eyes in a noble cause compared to letting down my two uncles who just happen to be my best buddies?

And so, despite the parental objections, I crest the twig and mud parapet, stuff two young crows into my pockets and recklessly plunge down that tree, leaving behind a considerable amount of boy-hide. As my feet touch ground, I am astonished to find myself still alive, let alone with eyes intact! Orlo, in awe of my feat, claims he actually saw sparks flying out of the seat of my pants during my earthward plunge. (Years later I go back, and finding the tree crashed to earth, examine it for both remnants of my skin and the crow's nest but find neither.)

I was thinking about this great escapade the other day when it suddenly struck me that the crows neither dive-bombed nor screeched at my downward scramble. I suspect they may have actually been relieved that I had reduced their tribe and thus their labours by half.

The crows have, of course, long since gone wherever crows go when they die. Gone, as well, are my mother and her father, both of whom were in the car with my sister and I that fateful day of the silent crows. The day my life and that of my sister, Phyllis, changed forever.

The school from which we were cruelly snatched still stands, red brick, squat, solid. The playground where we played endless games of "may I?" and "red light" now holds a tumbledown house. The shouts and laughter of little children are heard only in the memories of those of us who, carefree in our exuberant innocence, read our first stumbling words from Dick and Jane here.

Dick and Jane? I guess I had better explain that, since many of you won't know what I'm talking about. Dick and Jane with their little dog Spot are the lead characters in the book from which we learned to read when I started grade one.

This, of course, was long before computers or even television, if you can believe that! In fact, when I was a little boy, and really not so little, we didn't have electricity in our house. No indoor bathroom either! Unless you've actually "been there, done that," you have no idea how cold it is sitting over an oval-shaped hole cut in a board as the arctic wind whistles up your backside.

We did have a radio, though. I am certain it was the sight of my grandfather Henry Green, known to all as Dad, leaning his good ear into that old wooden radio, sucking up the latest war news, shushing silence into the boisterous brood crammed into the tiny kitchen, that led me to a career in broadcasting.

You know how sometimes a song or even a little bit of a song will keep playing over and over again in your head? Try as you might, you just can't get it out? That's the way it is with me and the little tune they used to play to introduce the six o'clock evening news on CFRB, beamed to us in Arthur from almost 100 miles away. Ta-da-da ta-da da de dum de dum de dum. Followed by the sonorous voice, I suspect, of Lorne Greene (no relation) announcing: "And now, CFRB Toronto presents the six o'clock news with Jim Hunter."

Uncle Willard, who is three years older than I, has a pretty good idea what is going on as Dad cups his good ear towards the crackling war-news radio. Even though he is also my uncle—the youngest of my father's brothers—only a few months separate Orlo and I, so we're too young to understand much. We know, though, from the grim faces at the radio during those early years of the war, that things are very bad indeed.

Grandma Green, whom we all called Mom, often wipes away a tear as Jim Hunter announces the casualties. Sometimes Dad sits there hunched in silence long after Mr. Hunter signs off. If the news is very bad he begins to pace. Back and forth his short legs take him. Past the scarred old red kitchen table and its eight wired-together and patched chairs. Back and forth.

We nervously watch, until finally, as a kind of signal to get on with our lives, he picks up the old metal dipper hanging at the side of our kitchen stove and begins ladling hot water out of the reservoir into the large dishpan.

Without electricity, the only way we can cook and heat the

house and water is with a wood stove that is the heart of every farm kitchen. Summer and winter, that stove must be kept fired up. We even cook our morning toast over it, the bread jammed onto a long metal fork Dad made in his little blacksmith's shop out behind the back kitchen. If we remove one of the stove lids and hold the homemade bread over the open fire at just the right height, and pay really close attention, sometimes we actually get real toast. Most of the time, though, it is just singed bread, usually more smoky black than brown.

The reservoir is a big water tank on the side of the stove that we boys are responsible for keeping filled at all times. This is where we get the hot water for our weekly baths, too, by the way! When Dad stops his pacing and grabs the dipper, it is a signal for all of us to clear away the remnants of supper and help Mom do the dishes and "clean up." Yes, we boys are just as responsible as my sister and our two aunts for housework. And it is supper we had when I was a boy on the farm. Dinner was served at noon. Go figure!

Well, you ask, if you didn't have electricity, how could you have a radio? Good question. The radio was powered by batteries: two smaller dry-cell batteries, as I recall, and a full-sized car battery we "borrowed" from our old Model T Ford. It was all hooked together with a rat's warren of wires. Don't ask me how it all worked. Uncle Cecil was a kind of genius when it came to stuff like that.

Once Cecil hooked up some kind of a generator to an old airplane propeller mounted on top of the roof. When the wind blew decently hard, not only did it power the radio, but a naked light bulb suspended over the kitchen table flickered off and on. You have no idea how exciting it was when the wind blew; the propeller actually spun and the bulb began to glow. I expect we got as much entertainment out of that little light bulb as kids do today with video games! It was a miracle, no doubt, but Dad always had a couple of coal oil lamps ready if the propeller didn't propel enough, which was most of the time.

One day in a high wind, the propeller gets spinning so fast it actually takes off from the roof and crashes into a field 122 yards away. I know it's 122 yards because Cecil measures it and the story is printed in our local newspaper, the *Arthur Enterprise*. Dad, with a twinkle in his eye, tells us very solemnly that we are very lucky indeed that the propeller didn't take the house with it. It is about as close to a lie as that dear man would ever come.

Now I don't want you thinking that airplane propellers grew in our backyard, or that you could just show up at the local Wal-Mart and buy one. In the first place, we didn't have a Wal-Mart. Nobody did.

Oh, we had stores in Arthur. Sussman's was Mom's favourite. You could buy almost everything there, from lye with which to make our own soap, to rubber boots, dresses and horse harness. About the only thing you couldn't buy at Sussman's was a car, although you could buy one of those from the Eaton's Catalogue!

I don't know what Mom would think if she could see Sussman's today. "The World's Biggest Men's Wear Store" is how they advertise themselves. They've taken over about half the main street of the little village, so there was obviously some money to be made in selling lye and rubber boots! But they didn't sell airplane propellers. We got ours on one of the most exciting days of my early life. All of this, of course, was before Phyllis and I were kidnapped.

I'm not sure how news flew around town so quickly in those days before local radio, daily newspapers or the Internet. Just the grapevine, I guess, which means, people just told each other the news.

The more exciting the news, the faster it spreads; and the faster it spreads, the more exciting it becomes. Thus by the time the news reaches us out there on the very edge of the village—Stumptown is what the people on snob hill call our end of town out near the railway tracks—the news one day is very exciting indeed.

Willard bursts into the house, red in the face and puffing wildly, having run the mile or so from town. "Mom, the Germans have attacked Arthur," he manages to gasp. "They shot down one of our planes!" For a six-year-old, this is about as exciting as it gets. I suppose it's pretty exciting news if you're 60! That is, if you believe it.

Mabel Green, having raised seven sons and two daughters, and semi-raised a grandson and granddaughter, is pretty hard to fluster. And obviously has some doubts as to the veracity of this breathless report. She gives Willard her best raised-eyebrow look. "Why would anybody bother attacking Arthur?" she asks. Willard is flabbergasted. His mother, having not only visited Toronto, but having lived in the United States, realizes that our tiny village of some two thousand souls is hardly a strategic target for Germans or anyone else. Willard, Orlo and I, on the other hand, know that Arthur is more or less the centre of the universe and likely the first place the Germans would attack.

"Well anyways, they sure shot down a plane at the dump, 'cause I saw it with my own two eyes," insists an indignant Willard. Forking his fingers over the bridge of his nose, he jabs just beneath the eyes he is referring to, in case she has doubts as to their existence as well.

As it turns out, Willard got a bit of it right. There is a plane down all right, but not from German bullets. Its balky motor conked out, right over Arthur's town dump, not a great place into which to crash or do anything else except shoot rats with a slingshot or, if you are from snob hill, with a BB gun.

Mind you, there are third and fourth generation Arthurites

who to this day, while grudgingly admitting the plane wasn't shot down, still talk darkly about sabotage. Hey, I just had a thought! Maybe the sabotage theorist's great-grandfather was the mechanic who was supposed to fix that motor!

I don't recall what happened to the pilot. I don't think he was badly hurt, other than probably a bruised ego. Imagine having to go through life with a flashing neon sign over your head saying: *I'm the guy who crashed his plane into the Arthur dump!*

One amazing thing was that even though the plane crashed headfirst into the dump, the propeller wasn't even bent. Must have been some awful squishy stuff he hit!

Dad's brother, known to everyone in our family as simply Uncle Bill, manages to get his team of Percherons into the dump, hitches a logging chain to the plane's carcass, and as he tells us later, "hauled her lock, stock and barrel to the wreckin' yard." It was there that Cecil pays 50 cents and lugs the propeller home, tied to the roof of his Model T Ford. He'd read in *Popular Mechanics* about how you could create electricity with a propeller.

When Dad sees him, as he says, "fiddlin' about" with the propeller and wires, he looks at him like he is crazy, but in his own quiet way encourages him. When that first joyous burst of electrical power surges down those wires to the radio, and that lonely little light bulb begins to flicker, Dad reaches over and gives Cecil's shoulder a little bit of a pinch. It is about as close to an open display of affection I ever saw from my kind and gentle grandfather.

He knows that Cecil, any day soon, might have to leave our little farm out here in backwater Ontario and march off to join the desperate fight to save us all from that madman Hitler. Dad is only too aware of what that could mean. Two of his brothers, Wes and Sam, marched off to fight the Hun in the First World War and were never heard from again. They were two of thousands of young men so swallowed up in the carnage called the Battle of the Somme that no trace of them could ever be found.

Some day when my grandchildren are a little older and can perhaps understand these things a little better, I will take them to Arthur and show them all that we have left to remember Wes and Sam Green. Two names etched into the cold, grey granite of the war memorial erected at the end of Main Street. A memorial to mark the end of the war to end wars. Or so we dreamed. You will find similar memorials in every hamlet, village, town and city in this country, but it would take you a very long time to read some 67,000 names.

Of all my grandfather Henry Green's nine brothers, Wes was my grandmother's favourite. One of the last times I visited her, before confusion overtakes her completely, she asks me to take her to see the memorial. Strangely, she doesn't get out of the car as we pull up in front of it. Just sits there for a moment, lost somewhere in the mist of memories. "You would have loved Wes," she says, pausing a moment. "He was the most like your grandfather." And then she turns to face me, face flushed, almost angry. "We fought for you and Phyllis, you know. We tried to get you back." And then in a sad whisper, "We all prayed."

It was the first time we had ever talked about it. All those years pretending it had never happened. I throw my arms around her frail shoulders. "I know. I know, Mom. It was a long time ago. It doesn't matter anymore."

. . .

Mary Ann

When I take that trip to Arthur with my grandchildren, the mood that settles over us that day will likely dictate which of two possible routes we take. The straight and narrow highway that shoots an arrow's path due west from Orangeville or the road that just sort of leaks north out of Guelph, dipsy-doodling its way, wandering around like a lost calf, until it butts up against the mighty Conestoga River. Cross the concrete bridge (mind the potholes, please) straddling the river which, except in spring, is usually just a muddy dribble, and there she is—all three blocks of magnificent Main Street! There can be no mistaken identity here; the giant green water tower, looming over the village like one of those Star Wars' long-legged monsters, shouts at you with huge black letters: ARTHUR.

I hope we're in a dipsy-doodle frame of mind the day we go because, to be honest, Arthur is not a place where you want to be in a hurry. Oh, it's true that this past few years a few real keeners haul themselves out of bed long before any self-respecting, early-bird rooster and head down that arrow path to Orangeville. From there, they plunge into the giant maw of hurrying humanity called Toronto. But for the most part, Arthur is the kind of place where, returning after a 20-year absence, people are likely to stop you on the street and remark how they haven't seen you in the past couple of months and how are things anyway?

There, still in the heart of Stumptown (only the old-timers still call it that, now that some of the nice people have pushed their homes to within hailing distance), we will find the house my great-grandfather Bill Green built with his bare hands. In that house, my grandfather Henry Green was both conceived and born.

Much later, my father lived in that house and so did I for part of two summers. That was years after we got the crows.

The war was over when finally Phyllis and I returned to Arthur. By then, Polly and Charlie had long since died, and Mom and Dad had sold their little farm about half a mile down the

Stumptown Road and moved to London. Willard and Orlo went with them.

When I show the house to my grandchildren, I will want them to pay special attention to the roof: two stories high, a very sharp peak, but still and all, pretty much a normal kind of roof. They shouldn't rush to dismiss it, though. If it hadn't been for that roof, they might not be here today, although I suspect love would have won out in the end, roof or no roof.

There is still much dispute in our family whether Mary Ann Gilder was 14, 15 or 16 when she ran away to marry Bill Green, son of Mollie Gillie, father unknown. She told Bill she was 16, but when pressed years later as to whether she hadn't stretched the truth a bit, all she would reply was, "Mind yer own damn business."

Lowell at the Arthur house his great-grandfather Bill Green built. It was onto that roof that his great-grandmother Mary Ann fled to escape her mother's wrath. His grandfather Henry Green was conceived and born under that roof.

Mary Ann's mother certainly didn't think she was old enough and came down the road with a switch after her. "You come home Mar Ann," she ordered, "or I'll whup ya." Mary Ann scrambled up onto the roof of the house Bill was building, that house you'll see right there. "Well, Ma," she said, "first you'll have to catch me!"

A few weeks later, Mary Ann Gilder and Bill Green were married. It is not clear if either one could read or write, but they raised a rollicking, hilarious pioneer family of which my grandfather, Henry Green, was the seventh of 10 sons. They had but one daughter who survived; another daughter died in childbirth. Henry never advanced beyond the fourth grade; the few pennies he could earn were vital for the family's survival in those days before welfare or unemployment insurance. He had the hands of a master craftsman and could make or repair anything, but his soul was that of a poet.

My father wrote a lovely book about Mary Ann and Bill Green entitled *A Time to Pass Over*. It is a delightful story of love, betrayal, triumph, tragedy and, above all, humour. A story that, if Hollywood wasn't so busy with blood and explosions, would make an Oscar-winning movie for the ages.

If ever you should visit the Arthur cemetery, you will see Mary Ann's gravestone, now adorned with a special plaque erected by the local town council recognizing her as one of Canada's pioneers, the heroine of my father's book. A heroine in more ways than one! Not satisfied with raising 11 children of her own, after Bill's death Mary Ann married a man named Henry Morden who had eight children.

Her beloved Bill was killed when a tree fell on him just before the turn of the century. They had been married 29 years. Mary Ann lived to the ripe old age (in those days) of 84. I was only two when she died in 1938, and thus have no memory of her. She had 58 great-grandchildren, of whom I am the eldest!

• • •

The Burial

Many of those who visit the Arthur Cemetery notice a strange indentation in the grassy knoll of the cemetery, not far from Mary Ann's grave. That it is so close to her gravesite is very appropriate, since she would have roared with laughter if she knew how that pockmark—that dimple—came to be.

It all began, according to my father who has documented the story in great detail in his book *Goodbye Little Town*, at the local hotel where one of my grandfather Green's brothers, named for some inexplicable reason Yankee, was known to hold frequent court.

My father used to tell me that if a Green could lick liquor, he could lick anything. He got it a bit wrong with Yankee who couldn't lick liquor but had no trouble licking anyone in town foolish enough to have a go at him. A famous drinker and scrapper was Yankee Green! Also a man who could be called upon to handle jobs no one else wanted, including, from all evidence, coming to the aid of more than a few lonely widows whose more attractive features had either never existed or had seriously deteriorated.

Thus it is only natural that Yankee is offered a couple of dollars and a couple of drinks to dispose of Sir Craigie, whose days as a magnificent Clydesdale stud were over. In his prime, Sir Craigie had been in great demand all the way to Guelph, Orangeville and beyond. The fruit of his loins were to be found pulling plows and wagons on dozens of farms. But came the time when Sir Craigie ceased to be interested in improving the Clydesdale race, and his owner found himself in need of a man who could handle sad emergencies of this nature. Yankee Green!

Nothing gains a man more friends more swiftly than free drinks. It was true then. It is true today. In very short order, Yankee finds himself surrounded by friends who, wisdom improving by the bottle, and remembering Sir Craigie's glory days, manage to convince him that being tossed into some miserable swamp to rot is hardly appropriate for a beast as grand as Sir Craigie.

Thus it is that when the drinks have finally run out, Yankee and several of his friends slip out of the hotel to the nearby livery stable where the unsuspecting Sir Craigie awaits to be quietly led out of town to the Protestant cemetery some two miles to the west.

"We'll bury him on hallowed ground," Yankee has decided. "Anyone who has led such a distinguished life deserves nothing less."

And so under cover of darkness, they dig a hole and lead Sir Craigie to its side. "Goodbye, old lad," they say. "Sorry to have to do this, but you've got to admit you've had an awful good life." And with one well-placed shot, they tumble Sir Craigie over into the grave.

The digging has obviously sobered them enough to spot the problem. The hole isn't deep enough. Try as they might to tuck them in, a good 18 inches of Sir Craigie's legs, topped by shiny hooves, stick up above the ground. They try heaping the earth up around them, but that doesn't work. It just keeps sliding away. They do their best, making a mound as high as some of the nearby tombstones over the incriminating appendages. Finally they borrow a wreath from a nearby gravesite, toss it on top and head back to town.

A town which is in an uproar the next morning. Someone has blown the whistle on Yankee. Some woman from snob hill claims she has absolute proof that Yankee Green has buried a horse in the Protestant cemetery and she demands immediate removal. "It is an outrage," she declares. Yankee pretends to be confused by it all. "I admit," he declares solemnly, "that Sir Craigie was owned by a Catholic. But you're forgetting Bobbie McTavish, who just happens not only to be Protestant but an Orangeman to boot, bred him. So how could you expect me to bury him in the Catholic cemetery?"

But Yankee has gone too far this time. Even the hotel keeper, who depends to no small degree on the patronage of Yankee and his friends, warns him that he has to do something. "Get that horse out of there, Yankee," he tells him, "or the constable will be after you and that's the truth."

Which is not to say that Yankee doesn't have his sympathizers. A lively discussion breaks out, centering around whether Sir Craigie wasn't more fit to be buried there than some of the humans. Several names are mentioned as possible exclusions, including that of a local bailiff, just recently deceased, who had foreclosed on Alfie Sherman's farm.

"Alright," agrees Yankee finally, "we've got to get poor old Sir Craigie out of there. How do we move a ton of dead horse anyway?" As you can imagine with the collective brainpower on display in the hotel that day, there are many suggestions. A block and tackle seems to be the best answer, but hauling a dead horse out of a cemetery with that kind of huge contraption, with half the town's population in attendance to critique the operation, would create an unseemly spectacle.

"Blast it all," says Yankee, "all I wanted to do was give the old boy a proper send off."

"Blast it," someone repeats. "That's the answer. Why not, Yankee? Why not blast him out of there?"

As luck would have it, among the many good Irishmen who lived in Arthur in those days was a man by the name of Mike Gainer. Mike was a farmer who had spent some time out in Montana somewhere, as a mule skinner he claimed. Don't be confused: a mule skinner is what they called men who drove mule teams, which pulled ore cars in mines. They made a whole television series, called "Death Valley Days," featuring mule skinners driving teams of 40 mules pulling giant carts across the desert. I don't think Mike Gainer was one of those; in fact, there's some doubt he had ever been to Montana, but he did have some dynamite and claimed to know how to use it.

"I'll blast the tops off the pyramids if you have the money to buy me the powder," he tells Yankee. "How much money you got?" "Five bucks," replies Yankee. "Do you figure that would buy enough dynamite to lift a ton of dead horse, say, five feet out of the ground?"

"Listen," says Mike, "you got five bucks and you got enough to blow that horse into so many smithereens that he'd never have to be buried at all. And probably have some money left over for a bit of celebration. Don't want to do it during the day, though," he adds. "I'm not really supposed to have this stuff, you know."

And so the deed is done that night. Mike sets his charges, calculating the amount of dynamite that he requires. Just to be on the safe side, he doubles the amount. He lights the fuse and they run for cover. Mike suggests that each remove his hat and clasp it to his breast in an attitude of prayer. "Not just to bid the Lord's blessing on Sir Craigie," he explains, "but because there might be enough dynamite under him to lift the whole kit and caboodle of us up with him!"

The resulting roar, so it is claimed afterward, can be heard in Kenilworth, eight miles away. Several nearby tombstones are tilted; a pane of glass is broken in a nearby barn.

Local legend has it that Sir Craigie simply disappeared, vaporized by the force of the tremendous blast. More likely he was buried on the installment plan. They had no time to fill the resultant crater, certain as they were that a lynching party was being rounded up and would soon be on its way.

Over the years, several attempts were made to level the ground, but for some strange reason after a few months the earth seemed to settle back in and the dimple you can still see would gradually re-appear. They finally gave up, the grass grew back over it, and that spot remains void of any human grave. People have long memories in Arthur! To the end of his days, Yankee Green claimed the dimple was the Good Lord's way of making sure that such a magnificent creature as Sir Craigie had something to mark his grave.

· · ·

Polly and Charlie

I'm not sure if it was just good luck or by design that those two crows we hijacked from that old elm tree down by the creek were old enough to survive away from the nest. I suspect Willard knew that you couldn't take a crow from its parents until they are fully feathered and almost ready to fly. If you kidnap them when they are still naked and mostly belly and mouth, they will likely die a shivering death a few days later. But when their feathers are all shiny and black and something in their tiny brain begins to shout, "flap those wings, it's flying time," they can make wonderful pets.

Curious, noisy and incredibly funny, it only takes a couple of days of feeding them before they begin following you around like wobbling little puppies. But boy, oh boy, do they eat! Wow! It was a good thing there were three of us and it was summer holi-days because it was pretty near a full-time job during those first weeks to keep them from driving us crazy with their squawking for more food.

Fortunately, young crows, and I presume older ones too, have marvellous digestive systems that allow them to eat just about any-thing. Worms, bugs and scraps from the kitchen table can be stuffed down their ravenous maws. This includes, as we learned, some of the stuff like onions that we hated and smuggled off our plates, into our pockets and out the door. The crows were noisily grateful for it all.

If there is a human within a mile, you can be certain a pet crow will get fed since there is no one, save perhaps the stone deaf, who could resist the frightful magnificence of their cawing for food.

Even after Polly and Charlie learned to fly and thus fend for themselves, they learned very quickly that hollering at a human got you a beak-full faster than poking around in the ground on your own. You'd be out working in the field (even I, aged six, had to help during haying and harvest) when one of them would land on your shoulder, loudly advertising a semi-empty stomach, even though it might have been filled only half an hour ago.

Harvest time was their favourite. Long before giant combines stalked the land, sucking in gallons of gasoline at one end while spitting bushels of grain out the other, we harvested with the kind of binders you now find in museums. Pulled by horses that pooped back into the furrows pretty much everything they consumed (the original recycling program), the binders cut the grain and tied it up into nice neat bundles we called sheaves. These sheaves couldn't be left on the ground, since the grain in them would soon rot or sprout.

If there were boys on a farm, it was usually their job to stack the sheaves into what we called stooks. It was kind of fun actually, especially if you had some buddies with you. You just stood the sheaves up on end and leaned half a dozen or so of them into each other into a kind of miniature teepee. If it was a really hot day and your dad or an older brother or uncle wasn't around, you could sneak into one of the stooks out of the sun and have a nice little snooze.

It was also a great place for mice to set up housekeeping. A beautiful, almost waterproof, golden ceiling offering shelter and a continuous meal. Safe, that is, until the grain and its stems (straw) had dried sufficiently for us to unceremoniously rip the roof from wee mousie's head and toss the sheaves into a wagon for its trip to the thrashing mill.

It doesn't take long for Polly and Charlie to discover that under many of these stooks awaits a lovely gourmet meal and a spot of entertainment. As you watch these black furies swoop down, fierce razor claws fully extended, pitiless screams of rage rocking fence posts, you understand that while the target is only a tiny mouse, for just a moment the crow might be a giant eagle on the attack!

The mighty raptors impatiently circle just a few feet overhead as we attack each stook with our pitchforks. Sometimes if the catch has been a little sparse that day, they plop down on your shoulder to urge you to better effort. The complaints are long and bitter at each stook that comes up dry. No doubt this is what Robert Burns had in mind when he wrote "Ode to a Wee Mousie." Had our two crows been able to talk, I have no doubt the poem eliciting sympathy for a mouse would have been met with snorts (caws?) of derision.

This business of crows being able to talk created a great deal of conjecture in Arthur.

One day a small scrum of boys scuffs its way down the Stumptown Road to our little farm wanting to see Polly and Charlie. One of them produces a wicked-looking jackknife and announces that he is going to help us all make a lot of money by getting our crows to talk. "All ya have to do," he assures us, "is just slit their tongues and they'll talk up a blue streak for ya." We've heard this before. In fact, Old Lady Anders, rumoured to be a distant relative and a little crazy, made a similar offer only a few days before, claiming to have accomplished the feat several times in the past. "It don't hurt them none," she assured us. "Just lets 'em talk like they was one of you."

Splitting crow's tongues to get them to speak was as commonly held a belief in those days as the one about never letting your cat near a Chinese restaurant! We weren't sure if it would actually work, and Willard said he doubted it very much, but for sure we knew it would hurt and no one was going to hurt our crows! We politely thanked Old Lady Anders, lest she put a curse on us, and sent the boys packing back down the road.

It is only natural then that in the fall the five of us head off for school together. Polly, Charlie and I are raw recruits. Willard and Orlo are the veterans, wise in the mysteries of formal education. The crows are indignant at being refused entry to the building, but are elated during recess and lunch at the prospect of sharing left-overs and unwanted crusts with dozens of screaming children.

A couple of the older boys, in older-boy fashion, think it is hilarious to peg apple cores at them. The crows have a ball. They execute a deft little two-step to avoid the missile, then snatch it up and—with a series of quick ducks of the neck and head flicks—down the hatch! Anxious for more!

Polly and Charlie faithfully follow us to school everyday, one full term with Willard, Orlo and me, then the following year for two months when Phyllis reaches that magic age of six and joins our little troop.

Four kids with two crows hovering, hiking down Main Street, Arthur, to school. What a sight that must have been! It's a wonder the *Toronto Telegram* or the *Star* didn't send a photographer up to show readers how quaint things were in the hinterland.

I still have a little article published in the *Arthur Enterprise* that tells how one sweltering afternoon, both of our crows flew through an open window, settling on Willard's desk, cocking their heads in as much bewilderment at the blackboard math problems as the rest of the class!

I presume they provided aerial surveillance for Willard and

Orlo for years after that. I don't know for sure. Phyllis and I weren't there anymore. The last time we saw Polly and Charlie was that brief glimpse from the floor of a car as it slunk guilty and ashamed out of town.

· · ·

Born Again

By any current standard, we were very poor growing up on that little Stumptown farm. By the standards of some of the nice people up on snob hill, we were not only poor but we were (roll of eyes, lift of eyebrow) Greens. "Oh," they would admit, "that Henry Green is an honest enough fellow, awful quiet too, and he can surely fix anything and never cheat you, but the rest of the family?!" Here there would be another roll of the eyes.

And it is true that you probably wouldn't want your daughter marrying one of Bill and Mary Ann Green's brood. Although, if the truth be known, there were more than a few daughters who in weaker moments were not averse to sneaking a few peeks at the powerful thighs, broad shoulders and thick chests most of the boys inherited from their father. "My Lord, those Green boys certainly were brawlers," I remember a woman telling my father, then wistfully, "but they sure were fun to look at!"

Aside from my grandfather and Wes, the brothers were great drinkers, scrappers, laughers, storytellers and pranksters. Which is why we didn't see much of them on our little farm. There was no drinking at our place, no smoking, no swearing, no card playing and—while there was lots of music and fun—no dancing either.

The only movies we were allowed to see featured hero dog Rin Tin Tin and the most famous singer of the day, George Formby.

George, as far as my grandmother was concerned, could do no wrong. If in a particularly good mood, she would flit around her kitchen humming the Formby hit song of the day "Roamin' in the Gloamin'," rolling out faux Scottish r's and g's in the best Formby impression until it would nearly drive you crazy, despite her fine voice. Good thing she never learned what kind of a rake old George really was!

Anderson, Indiana, 1911. Henry Green marries Mabel Hansen, the grandparents from whose home Lowell and Phyllis were abducted.

My grandparents' wedding picture, hanging on ancestors' row in our hallway today, reveals that Henry and Mabel Green were a very handsome couple indeed. My grandmother was a beauty, but if you look closely you will see that neither of them wore any jewellery, not even wedding rings, and my grandfather is shorn of a tie.

It had been revealed to elders of their church, apparently during their daily conversations with God, that adornment of any kind was a delight to the Devil. I doubt the young newlyweds believed that entirely, but it certainly helped them keep within their wedding budget of five dollars!

And that was an American five dollars! Let me tell you why. Most of the Green boys, if they wandered at all, would usually end up in a hotel someplace, but Henry was different. "Different from the day he was born," his mother Mary Ann claimed. "Not as much tomfoolery as the rest of them." So I suppose it was only natural that when Henry Green wandered, he ended up in one of those old-fashioned camp meetings you may have heard about. The kind where the preacher yells and screams, paces up and down the sawdust floor, the force of his warnings about hellfire and damnation enough to flutter the roof of the mighty tent glorifying Charlie Dingman's pasture.

'Til the day he died, Dad insisted that the night he answered the call from that preacher to come forward and be saved was the night his real life began. He would never try to push his religion on you, was in fact reluctant to talk about it, but if pressed would tell you that God spoke to him under the tent that night. "Called me to him and I went," he would say simply. It was a quiet and loving faith, which never wavered. One of the last things he said just before he died at the age of 98 was, "It's time for me to go now. I want to see Mom."

It was that faith that drew them together in the first place. The

Church of God was erecting a building at its headquarters in Anderson, Indiana, and needed some volunteer help. I'm not sure how he paid for the trip from Arthur. It is unlikely he had sufficient money of his own, but it was in Anderson that he met beautiful young Mabel Hansen, daughter of a mysterious Danish sea captain. Mabel was working for the church's publication *The Gospel Trumpet.*

They fell in love and married, and among the things God provided was my father! Several more children and many adventures later, they ended up back in Arthur where Henry Green bought a little Stumptown Road farm only about a half mile from the house in which he was born. It was on this farm that I spent some of the happiest days of my life.

· · ·

Mrs. Henry Green with her first-born, Gordon, Lowell's father, in Anderson, Indiana, 1912

This is the only picture we have of the Arthur farmhouse where Lowell spent so many happy hours. Left to right: Cecil, Gordon, Ken, Virgil's wife, Ethel, with their eldest child, Ruby, unknown, Virgil. In front are Lowell and Phyllis.

Above: Niles (Genevieve's son), Phyllis, Ruby, Virgil's daughter, unknown, and Lowell. Note the stylish backyard fence!

The three musketeers— Lowell, Orlo and Willard —with (probably) Niles

Grandma and Grandpa Green (Mom and Dad) with grandchildren. The baby in Mom's arms is probably Marielle, Lowell's half-sister who befriended Viola Lizzuio. No one is sure who that is in Dad's arms. Left to right: Niles, Ruby, Phyllis and Lowell. In front, Virgil's daughter, Audrey. That's Lowell's father's US Army hat Lowell is sporting.

All slicked up—
Phyllis and Lowell in
Ann Arbor, Michigan,
just prior to their
parents' divorce.

Of Stoves and Plows and Killdeers

Those of you who are raising or have raised a family, will have a good idea just how difficult it must have been for our grandparents to raise eight children and two grandchildren on only 80 acres of thin, rocky soil.

Eight of those mouths parked at the dinner table most nights belonged to the male of the species, and you have doubtless observed how many groceries they can put away in a single sitting! Mind you, in those days you really didn't need a lot of money. Not having much to buy or money to buy much with, was pretty standard on most farms just after the Depression.

You built your own house and barn. If you hadn't been wise or fortunate enough to grow a couple of boys along with the potatoes and corn, you got some neighbours to help. Their only fee was the understanding that you would be there when they needed a hand. The wood and the nails would probably be rescued from a neighbourhood building that had fallen over or burned down—the nails painstakingly flattened over an anvil or chunk of rail spurned by the CPR.

Every arm strong enough to hoist a hammer was pressed into action, and just like the blacksmith beneath the spreading chestnut tree, the arm either became a band of steel or pretty well fell off! At least that's what I used to claim. "Dad, one more of these nails and my arm's going to fall off," I'd say, as we prepared to add to our back kitchen. My grandfather would pause in his sawing, give my arm a brief glance and snort something like, "Huh, looks like a chicken arm to me." Which would spur me to whack away for another few minutes. There were few insults worse than being called a chicken *anything* around our place.

My grandfather made all our furniture—and if you discounted the esthetics (which you bet we did!)—kept it reasonably well-wired and nailed together. The pots and pans were hand-me-downs, sometimes so thin you could almost see the full moon through their bottoms.

The most important piece of equipment in any home, and the most expensive, was the kitchen stove, or range as we called it. Complete with overhead warming oven (great for drying mittens or flannel diapers), water reservoir and baking oven, it was such a remarkable engineering feat that the arrival of a new range was an event of considerable neighbourhood excitement.

Within minutes of arrival, the brawny delivery men would be swatting kids from underfoot as, red-faced and grunting, they hefted the mighty range from the back of the truck. By the time they had it in its place of honour in the kitchen, at least a half-dozen neighbours would just happen to wander in. And yes, in those days neighbours just wandered in any time of the day or night on any pretext. I do not believe any of the houses in Arthur, save perhaps the grand ones on snob hill, had locks, nor did we need them!

Only the arrival of a new baby engendered more interest, and come to think of it, the arrival of a new range was very much like a new baby welcome! Calloused hands caressing silky smooth metal skin, oven door opened for closer examination, nods of approval, sometimes a little wifely jealous jab of husband's ribs.

For Dad, the most important part of our old Findlay range was the oven door. It had to be strong enough and the right height to comfortably accommodate tired feet in need of toasting out the chilblains at the end of a bitter winter day. And just to give you an idea of how tired those feet must have been after many a day, consider this: Using a plow that gouged just one furrow at a time, required him to walk 10 miles for every acre plowed! Most years, he plowed 50 acres—500 miles!

Think of it! Each year, my grandfather, and many others like him, walked the equivalent of Ottawa to Windsor, or Ottawa to Toronto and about halfway back! Even when riding plows came along, some of them that would plow two furrows at a time, Dad refused, claiming it was just too much work for the horses.

Henry Green's plowing was cause for more than a little hilarity around town.

"What's the matter, Henry, fall asleep at the plow again?" Uncle Bill would chuckle at him, nodding and winking at my grandmother who didn't have a particularly good sense of humour to begin with and especially when her beloved Henry was the butt of a joke. She, of course, knew the truth. Plowed furrows are supposed to be straight. In fact, every year they hold what they call the International Plowing Match, where people win big prizes for having the straightest furrows.

But Dad's furrows always meandered a little bit, did a little loop-the-loop every once in a while, the kind of thing that might happen if you fell asleep for a moment or two and your horses were too stupid to walk in a straight line. With my grandfather, though, it wasn't sleep…it was killdeers!

I'm sure it won't be long until my grandchildren have their favourite actors. They'll probably plaster walls with their pictures, and avidly read all about their latest marriages and drug treatments.

When I grew up, most of us thought it was pretty hard to beat Roy Rogers, Marilyn Monroe or Gregory Peck, but my all-time favourite actor has to be the killdeer. Now before you think I'm having some kind of senior's moment, let me explain. Then you'll understand why my grandfather's plowed furrows were so crooked.

The killdeer isn't a particularly handsome bird. Its body is a little bit smaller and slimmer than that of a robin, but it has a set of long, toothpick-like legs and great big feet that make it look a bit like a giant insect. My uncle Virgil claimed they were called killdeers because flocks of them would attack and kill deer, but if you listen carefully you can hear it as plain as the nose on your face: "Kill deer, kill deer," they call to each other in a high-pitched, drawn-out cry. "Kill deer, kill deer," will come back the reply.

The first killdeer you see will probably have a broken wing. Maybe two broken wings which it will drag pitifully in the dirt. You will likely do everything in your power to catch the poor-suffering thing for an emergency rush to the bird hospital. But try as you might, just as you are about to catch the crippled bird it will manage to stagger an inch out of your grasp, its cries stark evidence of approaching painful death.

Then in a miracle rivalling the loaves and the fishes, the stricken killdeer will suddenly regain full strength, both wings will instantly heal, and with a loud "kill deer" which sounds very much like a jeer, it will vault into the air, laughing I am certain!

By sheer coincidence, her wing-dragging path has taken her and you far from her nest hidden somewhere near in the grass. The "miracle cure" occurred just as her four fluffy little chicks managed to scurry into deep cover under a bush. Can your favourite actor beat that?

I'm going to slip in a little bit of biology here. You can skip this part if you want, but if you read it you will know something few people are aware of.

Baby killdeer, like baby chickens and ducks, come out of the egg running. They hatch with their eyes open, and as soon as their downy feathers dry, they start scurrying about, following their parents and searching for food. Newly hatched killdeer, just as with chickens and ducks, can't fly. They still need their parents to look after them, but they are a lot closer to independence than most baby birds.

Crows, for example, and robins and blue jays are born almost naked, blind, bald, like wrinkly skinned little lizards, and quite frankly hideous. Baby killdeer are cute and fluffy. Baby crows and robins are so ugly it's a wonder their parents don't kick them out of the nest!

Baby birds that hatch cute are called precocial, which means "ripened beforehand." Baby killdeer, chickens, ducks and quail don't just lie in their nest being waited on claw and wing, they're out and about almost at birth.

Birds that hatch blind, naked and helpless are called altrical, which comes from a Greek word meaning "wet nurse." These birds lie helpless, relying on their parents to not only bring them food but push it down their throats—and in some cases even partially digest it first. Ugh! These ugly altrical birds remain in the nest at least two weeks before they can leave; even after that, their parents are usually still feeding them, sometimes for an entire summer.

Cute birds (precocial) stay in the egg twice as long as the ugly birds (altrical) so they have more time to develop before they poke their heads out of the shell. A one-day-old killdeer or chicken is actually two weeks older than a one-day-old robin. Even though adult robins and killdeer are about the same size, the killdeer's eggs are about twice the size of robins, which means there is more for the baby killdeer to eat inside the shell.

So now maybe you can understand why it was that Grandfather Green refused to plow over a killdeer's nest in the field. That's why his furrows wove around and about. Each time he saw a killdeer going into its broken-wing act, he knew there was a nest nearby. When he spotted it, he would instruct the horses to "gee" a bit to the right or "haw" to the left, leaving the nest safe and sound. After a while, Old Bill and Queenie got so they could spot a killdeer nest on the ground and would swing around it without instructions!

• • •

The Sleepy R

One of the advantages of being a little kid is that you're built very close to the ground, which when picking bugs from potato plants or stones off the ground is a major advantage. No surprise then that those were two jobs that Orlo and I were often assigned to. In fact, picking potato bugs was our first paid employment. A penny per 100 bugs, as I recall, was the going rate. One thousand bugs dropped into a little can of coal oil and we had enough for an ice cream Melo Roll each!

Picking rocks was much harder, but for some reason, I don't recall ever being paid for that. Given the preponderance of rocks on our farm, perhaps it was felt picking a thousand was just too easy. It didn't seem to matter how many we plucked from the fields and planted along fencerows, the following spring the frost would heave another abundant harvest to the surface and we would start all over again.

The best stone spotter on the farm was Old Bill, who without aid of any direction, would drag the stoneboat from rock to rock and patiently wait while we tossed it aboard. Sadly, while obviously a very smart horse, we never could get Old Bill trained to pick the darn things up. Perhaps he was smarter than we knew!

Dad actually enjoyed stone picking, probably because he was always on the lookout for Indian arrowheads and meteorites. I don't recall him ever finding an arrowhead (what self-respecting Indian would be camping in a field near Arthur anyway?), but he did once find a cabbage-sized meteorite that became one of his prized processions, and remains in the family today. Cecil, I believe, has it. Nonetheless, there was something about stone picking that always prompted the only self-doubt I ever heard my grandfather express. "Don't know why I bought a farm with all these rocks and no bush," he would grumble to himself. It was a good question.

Given the tremendous amount of wood required to keep a house warm during winter, the lack of a large woodlot was a serious handicap on any farm. Buying wood required the one thing we had very little of—cash.

I'm not sure who came up with the solution. I do recall Mom telling us that we must never tell anyone what we were doing. Not because it was wrong, because using what others were wasting was clearly not the least bit sinful, but as proud as she was, she wanted no one to think that we were so poor we could not afford to heat our own home. And so the three of us, Willard, Orlo and I, found ourselves with new unpaid employment. Because of the warning, this at least was a job with a little bit of intrigue.

Equipped with old feed bags, we set out each morning in search of unburned coal along the CPR railway track which runs right behind our farm. It is an especially lucrative search immediately following the fierce snowstorms that sweep across that part of central Ontario that lies in the lee of the inland ocean called Lake Huron. Winds whipping across the northern Michigan peninsula soak up tons of moisture on their journey across the lake, and then dump a terrible mess right on our doorstep each winter.

There must have been something peculiar about the topography of our farm, because inevitably after each storm, a huge snowdrift, often six or seven feet high, blocked the railway track directly behind our barn. Sometimes they hooked two locomotives together, attached a huge plow to the front and smashed through that drift and many others like it along the line. I recall on more than one occasion the mighty engines having to back up several times and take flying runs at our drift before they finally plunged through. When that happened, repair crews would come chugging up the track on their little pump cars, very often the next day, to replace a stretch of rail that had been damaged by the spinning locomotive wheels.

As you can imagine, this energetic ramming often jolted large quantities of coal off the coal car onto the snow. If we managed to get there before the repair crews, we could often score several full bags. The pickings weren't as good during summer, but I suspect that kind-hearted firemen and engineers often just "accidentally" tossed a shovelful or two over the side as they passed farms like ours. I am certain we were not the only ones in those days with a "secret."

As you probably know, CPR stands for the Canadian Pacific Railway, but around Arthur when I was growing up, everyone knew it as the "Sleepy R." For good reason. The 20-mile trip from Orangeville to Arthur would take the better part of an afternoon.

You've heard the expression "a milk run"? Well, the Sleepy R is where the phrase must surely have started. From Orangeville, through Arthur, Kenilworth and Mount Forest to the end of the line at Teeswater, the old Sleepy R picked up milk cans left on little trackside platforms at dozens of farms.

Starting from a dead stop required an incredible amount of huffing, puffing, shuddering, jerking and complaining for beat-up old steam engines relegated to milk-run duty during the war years. It didn't take the engineers long to perfect the art of slowing down at each milk stop just enough for a strong-armed man to drop yesterday's emptied cans onto the platform, grab the full ones, and haul them aboard while the train was still moving.

I recall a trip when a soldier in full dress uniform jogged alongside the train for several miles. When he swung back in, he boasted he hadn't even worked up a sweat!

But milk and the odd passenger with time to kill wasn't the only freight the Sleepy R transported. Gasoline and tires were severely rationed. Trucks were rare, so most of the town's supplies had to be shipped in by Sleepy R trains.

Each Monday, there arrived alongside the dry goods, plows, horse harness and new kitchen ranges several large wooden barrels of beer. Depending upon the thirstiness of Arthurites, these barrels would sometimes sit for several days in a large storage room attached to the Arthur train station, awaiting a summons from the Commercial Hotel.

The fact that good beer might sit unappreciated for several lonely days in a railway station was a great affront to the finely tuned sensibilities of Arthur's leading philosophers. They had discovered, as had others before them, that there was a definite correlation between acuity of thought and debate and the amount of alcohol consumed. The more alcohol, the more profound the Socratic discussions that followed.

Thus it was that one fine Monday morning, a couple of the Green boys, we think Yankee and Frank, although neither of them ever confessed, find themselves at the train station. The station master, while adept at Morse code on the telegraph, is ill-prepared to deal with artists of deception as skilled as my great uncles.

"Now I understand," says one of them, "that Art Fennel has bought himself a new milk separator. I've got to get myself one of those and I was wondering if you might open up the storage room here so we can have a look at the latest thing the smart boys have come up with." The station master, unaware that neither of them had ever milked a cow in their lives, complies. One of the brothers distracts the poor fellow, while the other paces off the distance from the beer barrels to the front and side of the storage room.

That night several men lugging washtubs, flashlights and a brace and bit watch as one of the Green brothers crawls beneath the storage room, does some measuring and announces, "Gimme the brace and bit, boys, she's right over my head." And he is right! A few energetic cranks of the brace and bit, and the floor is breached; a few more cranks, and something begins to trickle down. As expert as they are in this type of identification, there is no hesitancy in declaring they have a gusher—and on the first try. To their credit, only one barrel is drained. As one of them says, "It would be an awful thing if the Commercial went dry on us this week."

Years later, after he had given the villagers many other shenanigans to chuckle about, came the time Yankee had to choose between the two rival cemeteries for his own burial. The doctor gave him at most a week.

"I've had a wonderful life," says Yankee, "but the wife is going to be some awful upset. Could you break the news to her?"

Yankee's wife is Irish Catholic in a time when the idea of dying outside "the Church" strikes terror into the hearts of the faithful. Her beloved husband is going to die outside the faith. It is the one terrible fear of her life now coming true. He will have to be accompanied to the Protestant ceremony only by the Anglican minister. Any hope that she would meet up with him in Heaven is shattered.

Yankee pleads with her not to be frightened, but it is painfully clear that she will live the rest of her life in abject fear. "Well," says Yankee, as the time ticks away, "I never figured I'd go out asking anyone for anything, but I've got to do it. I cannot leave my poor wife like this. Call for the priest."

And so it is that the very last thing Yankee Green does is to become a Catholic on his deathbed. The Anglican priest is told his services are no longer required, and Yankee is buried in the Catholic cemetery with all the benefits that entails. An act of supreme kindness from a man many in Arthur wouldn't say hello to if they met him on the street.

The story doesn't end there. My father says that about 30 years later, his good friend Cornelius Callaghan told him that as the undertaker in charge of the funeral, he had been called upon to make a rather unexpected defense of Yankee's deathbed conversion. This defense had to be made to a doubting Protestant—an especially upright and proper Presbyterian named Billy Oakes. Billy, it seems, was working at the cemetery at the time of Yankee's death. Helping to dig and tend graves.

According to Cornelius, he and Billy were on their way to check on Yankee's grave when Billy began to question him about the last-minute conversion to Catholicism. "Now you mean," asked Billy "that after all the hellraising and such that Yankee did all his life, that when he's ready to pass through the Pearly Gates, just by calling a priest, all is forgiven and Yankee can spend eternity in Heaven? You don't think that a conversion like Yankee's was just a bit too convenient and a mite too late?"

Cornelius answers the question by referring the doubting Billy to the Good Book itself. "You remember how it was with Our Lord when He was being crucified? How Our Lord turned his head to the thief who had just repented of his sins and promised him that "this day thou shalt be with me in Paradise"? Billy nods.

"Yes," says Cornelius, "I do believe old Yankee has made it to that Promised Land."

Billy sits there for a long time, taking it all in. "You don't believe me," says Cornelius. "Yes," replies Billy, "I guess I have to."

"Well, what are you looking so sad for and shaking your head?"

"Well," says Billy quietly. "I was just thinkin' about all the fun I never had all these years, all I've been missin' and probably didn't have to at all."

• • •

The 12 Days of Root Beer

How would you like a bottle of ketchup as your big Christmas present? The idea is probably so foreign you cannot even contemplate it. If all you got under the tree on Christmas morning was a pair of hand-knitted socks and a big bottle of ketchup, you'd probably think seriously about packing up and moving in with the neighbours. But a bottle of ketchup is what Willard asked for one year, and when he got it, he claimed it was the best present he'd ever received.

Things are about as tough as they can get that winter of 1942. The crops have been poor, the world is just emerging from the terrible Depression, the war is going badly, and the Green family has two new mouths to feed. Phyllis and I have fled a crumbling marriage and found refuge with loving grandparents.

My father's education and the two jobs he toiled at to support us have been interrupted by a call from the United States Army (he was born in Anderson, Indiana, don't forget). Uncle Sam desires his services, and he somehow manages to convince them that with two years of medical school at McGill he is an expert on tropical diseases. What he ends up as is an expert in diseases not necessarily restricted to the tropics. "Short-arm inspection" in the Texas desert is how he always described it to me.

The ten dollars a month per child the US Army proudly ships off to our Stumptown farm to pay for our keep is about all the cash available in our household. So, early in December, we get the news. "Well," announces Mom, "guess what? This year we're going to be able to buy each of you a special present." Pointing to Eaton's Catalogue, she continues. "Pick two or three items under two dollars each. Tell us what your choices are, we'll pick one of them, then on Christmas morning it will be a surprise." As you can tell, my grandmother was the eternal optimist and a great sales lady.

Both Orlo and I dive into the catalogue and come up with a list of several items, but Willard doesn't need Eaton's help. "I want a bottle of Heinz ketchup," he insists, and cannot be dissuaded.

Come Christmas, I get a metal windup bulldozer, Orlo gets a set of pick-up sticks, but no one is as excited as Willard when he opens his present and there it is: a large-sized bottle of Heinz ketchup. He whoops for joy, and for the next several days pours it over everything, pancakes included. His favourite is ketchup sandwiches! (If my grandchildren try one, I hope they don't tell their mothers they got the idea from me!)

There is a special treat that Christmas. My father sends us a dozen oranges from his army camp in Texas, and amazingly enough they all arrive with their peel still intact. He has cleverly packed the oranges in a box marked "Medical Syringes," something obviously no one along the route has any need for. Oranges, on the other hand, are an extremely desirable and rare luxury in 1942. Had the real contents of that box been discovered en route, it is highly probable that all that would have arrived at the Arthur train station would have been an empty box.

Christmas, even with two-dollar gifts and a lonely orange poked into the toe of a stocking hung over your bedpost, was just as exciting for a kid in those days as it is today. Just all being together was fun, and always when the Greens got together there was music.

Just to give you an idea of how special it was, Mom would open up the parlour, something reserved for weddings, funerals and, on occasion, courting. (Orlo and I spent hours one day giggling and peeking through the keyhole as my Uncle Ken and his soon-to-be-wife Jimata held hands and even kissed on the parlour sofa.)

But on Christmas Day, Mom opens this hallowed ground to us all. She or Aunt Nilah, visiting all the way from Toronto, sit down at the piano; if my father is there, he toots away on the saxophone,

Cecil plays the guitar and banjo, so does Virgil, and we sing along. Aunt Genevieve keeps us in stitches with her jokes. We don't need money to be happy—which is a very good thing since we don't have any!

But for all the joy that Christmas brings, for sheer anticipation and pure enjoyment, there is nothing to compare with the 12 days of root beer.

Has this kind of thing ever happened to you? You're sitting there, in a park, in a restaurant, maybe driving around or just walking down the street, and it hits you right in the heart. A sudden warm, very loved, safe kind of feeling, like maybe your mother has just kissed a bo-bo better or your airplane is safely down after a terribly bumpy ride. There won't be any apparent reason for the feeling. It just kind of floods you like a sudden sunny ray, then just as quickly disappears. It may happen only once, or many times. You may discover the cause or it may remain a mystery.

This will probably sound crazy, but I used to get that warm rush of good feeling every time I walked into the Cathay Chinese Restaurant on Albert Street in Ottawa. And don't laugh and say, sure, that's because you like Chinese food so much. It's true, I certainly do like Chinese food. Truth is, I like most food (except onions), but there was something about the Cathay that gave me a warm little tickle at the back of my memory. I couldn't figure it out until I took my father there for lunch one day.

We are no sooner seated than I see him looking at the bar strangely. "What?" I ask. "What do you see?" He pauses a moment. "Those bright-coloured balls on top of the liquor bottles." He points to the unique jiggers for measuring shots of liquor, which still adorn the Cathay's bar bottles. "They look just like the Christmas tree decorations I bought in Ann Arbor right before your mother and I broke up."

By this time we both know he is dying, the blood transfusions administered to battle leukemia less effective each time, so I do something I never would have under different circumstances. I reach out and cover his hand with mine. "You loved her, didn't you?" He nods slightly. "But that Christmas was really for you and Phyllis," he says. "I knew it would be the last with the four of us together. The war was on, your mother was making threats about leaving and taking both of you with her. I was afraid I might never see either of you again." He pauses for a moment, then gives a little chuckle. "So I went out and, like a damn fool, spent every cent we had on decorations and presents, which of course made your mother even madder."

As strange as this sounds, I have some understanding of my mother's anger. My father, whose own childhood had been stunted by the responsibilities heaped on the shoulders of the eldest of a large brood in desperate times, spent his entire adult life in an almost childlike pursuit of decorations and presents. When he died, he had an entire second house filled to bursting with "things" he had acquired over the years. Everything from a jar filled with mud from the bottom of the well Phyllis was digging at her Brantford home, to a human skull he had somehow (probably illegally) acquired at McGill Medical School.

His barns were filled with strange-looking exotic chickens, sheep, dogs, goats, and at one time even a buffalo. In his fields with their ramshackle fences, roamed even more exotic Belted Galloway cattle that looked like Oreo cookies. Presents and decorations! His books for the most part, while beautifully written, created a kind of fantasy world of small-town life where neighbours were all wonderful characters looking out for each other, and every story had a happy ending.

And right now, he wants a happy ending. "Hey," he says, taking his hand from mine. "Let's see if they've got any Hires Root Beer!"

Now there is a really happy thought!

As luck would have it, they do have root beer. Better yet, Hires. "And we don't have to wait 12 days for it," he grins. He takes another sip. "Not bad, not bad. But not as good as the stuff we used to make, eh Buggerlugs?" He laughs aloud. Buggerlugs! It is a name he hasn't called me in what? Fifty years, I guess!

The 12 days of root beer starts with sugar. I forget how many pounds we needed, and for the life of me, I can't find anyone who can recall the exact recipe. What I do remember is that all of us kids had to forgo sugar on our oatmeal for several months before we had enough to make root beer. Those were the days when sugar was rationed.

During the war, every household in Canada received little booklets of ration coupons for a number of food items. Living on a farm, the only one that really affected us was sugar. It was about the only thing we couldn't grow or produce ourselves.

Mind you, our sugar deprivation wasn't as serious as it might have been if we had owned a car. Gasoline was rationed along with many food items, but since the only horsepower we had was the four-legged kind, my grandfather Green had no difficulty trading our gasoline coupons for sugar coupons.

Cecil usually had an old Model T Ford kicking around (or parts of several) for which he needed gas, so some of the coupons were usually just traded over the supper table. One pound of sugar for one gallon of gas was the usual formula. Cecil complained that this wasn't really fair since his Model T burned up a gallon of gas a lot faster than we burned up a pound of sugar. To which Dad would usually harrump something like, "Well, if you didn't drive that thing so fast, you wouldn't burn so much gas." Keep in mind, please, top speed for a Model T was about 25 miles an hour!

A Model T, by the way, was the only vehicle Henry Green ever learned to drive. Years later, when Cecil showed up at Mom and Dad's 50th wedding anniversary with a Model T he'd "rescued" from some farmer's barn, my grandfather rose to our challenge. He escorted his blushing bride of 50 years into the passenger seat, hopped behind the wheel, got Orlo to crank her up, and away they chugged up the dusty road to mighty cheering and much joking about whether the chauffeur would remember where the brake was.

That was the year my father and his new love and soon-to-be-wife Cheryl showed up from Quebec with a brand new Buick and a pet raccoon which, according to Cheryl, had been fully house-broken. She was correct. The raccoon did not poop in the new Buick. Instead, as we watched the anniversary couple open their presents, Mr. Coon treated himself to the rubber mouldings around the car windows, and would have finished off the seats had he not been rudely interrupted by an ungodly roar.

I'd heard that roar a few times before. In particular, the time George the ram caught my father looking the wrong way and butted him bum over tea kettle, and again when a cow he had just rescued from a muddy ditch pinned him against the tractor. It was a roar my father reserved for animals he was really, really mad at.

Cheryl recognized the roar, as well. She sprang from the picnic table we were seated around and dashed to the car. "Gordon! Gordon! Don't touch that raccoon! Gordon! Gordon!"

She need not have worried. If my father had caught that raccoon, heaven only knows what he would have done. For that matter, heaven only knows what the raccoon might have done to him. But even in the confines of the Buick, the raccoon was too quick and too smart for any human. The coon timed it perfectly. Cheryl opened the passenger door just a crack. "Gordon, leave him

H. Gordon Green and Lowell's stepmother, Cheryl, on their wedding day

alo—." Four paws and 40 pounds of mask and striped tail hit the
door, slamming it against her shins and almost knocking her down.

As the saying goes, the coon was last seen heading for the hills!
When we all finally managed to stop laughing, Mom and Dad
claimed watching the whole thing was the best present of all.

Actually, it was a special present for my grandfather that had
prompted my father to go back to the car and thus save most of the
Buick's seats. Just as with cars, my grandfather's taste in soft drinks
hadn't changed in 50 years either. He loved the root beer we brewed
on the farm, and while he claimed the new stuff wasn't nearly as
good, he could sock back two or three bottles of it at a single sitting
and look around for more. It had to be Hires, of course. It was
Hires extract we used to make the "Chez Stumptown" stuff, and he
was convinced nothing else came close.

They came out with a brand called Dad's Root Beer once, and someone thought it would be cute to present him with a couple of cases. He wouldn't even open them! He grumped a bit for awhile that no one was making homebrew anymore, but when one of his sons jokingly told him that if he wanted to wait 12 days, his eldest son Gordon was willing to make him some, my grandfather gave him a searching look and held out his hand for the six-pack of Hires that Willard was carrying. My father's ability to turn home-made root beer into vile swill was legendary!

My grandfather made it pretty plain that if we weren't going to make some decent homebrew, his children were responsible for keeping him stocked up with an acceptable substitute, so on each birthday or other special occasion, he usually ended up with enough Hires to keep him going for a couple of months.

A 50th wedding anniversary was certainly a special occasion, so in the space not occupied by the raccoon, my father had loaded about 20 cases of Hires' best, along with a few bottles of Spruce beer, which Dad had recently declared wasn't half bad. The family consensus was that had my father not gone to get those bottles when he did, the raccoon would have completely devoured the interior of the car. Ken suggested he might have polished off the engine, as well, block and all.

It is true my father simply could not make root beer. But then, he had difficulty driving a nail, or a car for that matter! But my grandfather certainly had the knack. The little bottle of Hires extract, the sugar, the fresh well water, the little blocks of yeast, all measured carefully into sterilized preserving jars, then hauled lovingly down to the basement to sit and brew for 12 days. Undoubtedly, the longest 12 days in history. We all kept special calendars, marking each day off carefully.

Of course, it required constant supervision. First thing after school, down to the basement to check on the brewing root beer. Great excitement when the first tiny bubbles appear. We dash up the stairs, shouting, "It's starting, it's starting." Everyone knows what we mean. We watch fearfully for any sign of mould or cloudiness. Henry Green's record of successful brewing is exemplary, but we know the risk involved. We've all heard the horror stories of entire batches going bad. Aside from my father's, of course. His attempts aren't considered serious by any of us.

Even under my grandfather's careful hand and watchful eye, sometimes a jar or two would, for no apparent reason, turn sour. Once a jar exploded, and for days afterward we jumped at any sudden sound, fearful the whole batch might blow up like one of those bombs they were dropping on London.

And then finally the 12th day. Excited anticipation mixed with apprehension. "Well," Dad says, "guess we'd better see if that root beer is any good, eh?" He should have been on the stage. Down the cellar steps he descends. No one is allowed to accompany him. It is far too delicate a task. Tinkle, tinkle, we can hear as he moves the jars around. "To find the best one," he claims, but it is surely intended to prolong the drama. Then, ever so slowly…tramp, tramp, tramp, up the stairs, cradling a precious jar in his arms. "Mom, I think we need a glass here." It is in front of him in a flash. Slowly the lid is unscrewed and set carefully on the table. Dad peers into the jar, lowers his nose and sniffs loudly several times. "Looks okay, smells okay. Let's give her a little taste."

Was there ever a wine steward with a better performance? An inch or two carefully poured into the glass. Held up to the light, swirled around a few times, sniffed again, then ever so delicately glass to lips, tipped back even slower. Finally, the Adam's apple bobs. The glass is empty. We wait breathlessly. Dad looks to the ceiling, tilts his head a bit to one side, then the other. "Well," he says, "I guess it will have to do." There is enough cheering to make the Queen wave!

I have eaten in some of the finest restaurants in the world. I have sampled some of the finest and most expensive wines in the world, but I swear nothing, but nothing, has ever tasted as wonderful as that first sip of "Chez Stumptown" root beer.

My grandfather was right: the newfangled stuff in fancy bottles and cans isn't bad, but it doesn't hold a candle to the homebrew we used to make back on the farm. If I can find the recipe and if they still sell Hires extract, we'll make a batch when my grandchildren are old enough to help. But I'll have to warn them: they'll have to wait 12 days!

. . .

The Pork Chop Story

When my daughters and Jeremy were little, very few weeks passed without one of them insisting that I tell them the pork chop story. "Tell us your pork chop story," they would say through their giggles. I'm not sure what intrigued them so much about that particular story. Maybe it was because I was about their age when it happened, or it might have had something to do with the idea of this grown-up man getting into trouble for something they could imagine themselves doing.

By the time I had related the story a dozen or more times, they could recite it themselves—word for word. Indeed, if I dared change the story by a single word or even inflection, they would gleefully shout the correction until it became a game. "Tell us the pork chop story," they would shout, and eagerly wait until I purposely gave it a different twist. Their eyes would light up as they jumped in with the correct version.

By now you have an idea how poor we were growing up in Arthur and you've probably got a pretty good idea that our family was very religious. No playing cards, no jewellery, no dancing, and of course, only "Rin Tin Tin" and "George Formby"! We never minded; in fact, as far as we were concerned we had just about the best life of anyone on the planet. Kids running all over the place with no one telling us we couldn't climb trees or go swimming in the nearby creek.

We couldn't have scraped together a dime among the four of us, but we were as free as the wind, unencumbered by rules or adults. We made up our own games and roamed the countryside. Adventure lay just over the next hill.

We had jobs to do, but for the most part we experienced the kind of freedom children today can only dream about. Get your chores over as quickly as possible, stuff your pockets with Mom's fresh homemade bread, then disappear until supper. No one ever worried about us. No one even asked us where we had been or what we had done, but you can be sure we never missed supper, because by then we were hungry enough, as Willard used to say, to "eat the rear end out of a skunk." He'd only use words like that, you understand, well away from the house or adults. "Rear end," or anything approaching it, around the Green household would likely get you one fast trip up the stairs and to bed "misterman." And no dessert!

Supper was a wonderful, warm family time in our house. Mom insisted that we all sit down together, often by the warm light of coal oil lamps, and no matter how bad the crops might have been that year, we never went hungry. "Plenty of nothing fancy," was how my grandmother would describe it. But before you were allowed to touch a morsel, heads were bowed, eyes closed, lips zipped and Murphy the mutt, lurking beneath the table, toe-jabbed to silence.

In the Green household, no matter what struggles we had

endured to put food on the table, there was no question as to the identity of the real provider. "Thanks be to God," we would all say. Then my Grandfather would begin that wonderful and now almost ignored ritual—grace. I'm not sure if grace is forgotten today or if there just isn't much of an opportunity. Few of our new and much improved nuclear families ever sit down together for a meal, unless it's at the McDonalds' drive-through, and besides which, how many families would even know a grace to say?

In our house, the honour of saying grace was reserved for my grandfather. His years of experience equipped him beautifully for the job, except for one thing. As with many experts in their field, he had perfected the art of protraction. No one could stretch grace out longer than Henry Green could.

Especially during those early war years, it wasn't sufficient to simply ask God's blessing on the food we were about to eat. That was an afterthought. What Dad really wanted was to get in some gentle nudging about the war and his sons who were either off fighting or might soon be called up. As well, there were usually a few little hints about getting the Government up there in Ottawa to (God willing) smarten up!

In the spring, a word or two about needing dry weather for seeding would be squeezed in. If it were summer, God would be kindly reminded of the need for rain. In the fall, the biblical phrase "bountiful harvest" would usually creep in. Living in the famous snowbelt as we did, there were plenty of requests that if it was God's will we would all appreciate it if the storm missed us this time. Once, I recall, he even managed to mention the fact that the last two big storms had skipped Fergus but plugged our roads for days.

All the while, we are hunched over our plates, forks poised in attack mode, stomachs grumbling like distant thunder, trying not to get caught sneaking peeks at the promised delights which, if and when grace ever finished, we might actually get to sink our forks into.

I don't want you ever to breathe a single word of this, but my nickname when I was a little boy was "gag pot." I'm not sure who started it. Probably Willard, but that's the cross I had to bear for several years. Gag pot! Can you imagine?

It was all because of onions. I could not stand onions. Could not stand the sight of them, the smell of them, and especially the taste of them. In those days you had no choice. You had to eat everything on your plate. You were not allowed to not like anything. Food was food, and any refusal to eat on the grounds you hated it was unacceptable. Not liking food was a luxury we could not afford. My problem was, I simply could not eat onions. My valiant attempts inevitably ended in a serious bout of gagging which, of course, Willard and Orlo thought was hilarious. Hence the moniker "gag pot." A warning: If anyone today tries to sneak onions into my stew or salad, they could be in big trouble. And this includes all members of my family!

So if onions, or even carrots which I wasn't crazy about either, were on the night's menu, waiting for Dad to wrap up grace wasn't that onerous. On the other hand, a pile of pork chops staring us down was a different story! Waiting through an indeterminable grace before being allowed to attack a pork chop was pure torture. I absolutely adored pork chops. Especially in the dead of winter, when we were pretty well living on stale potatoes and salt pork, and hadn't had any fresh meat for a couple of months.

Today, if you want a little snack, you open the fridge door and poke around until something hits your fancy. Okay, what would you do if you didn't have a fridge? Presents a problem you never thought of, doesn't it? You probably think refrigerators have always existed, just like telephones, television and flush toilets, but the fact is none of those things were available to us when I was a boy.

I suppose a few of the people up on snob hill may have had an indoor flush toilet and maybe even a telephone, but refrigerators could only be found in really rich people's homes until after the war. A few families in big cities had iceboxes, cooled with huge blocks of ice delivered door to door every day, but that was far too expensive for most farm families. We relied on Mom's "preserves," the root cellar, the well, salt and, in winter, ice and snow to preserve our food.

Summers were glorious feast times. A few steps outside our back kitchen lay a wonderland of fresh vegetables and fruit. Butter (my job to churn that!) and milk were cooled by suspending them on a platform halfway down the well. As devilishly clever as they were at hiding their eggs, the hens that roamed the barnyard couldn't outsmart three boys, so we had fresh eggs each day.

Sweet corn grew like Jack's beanstalk, almost as high as an elephant's eye! One year, Cecil won the family corn-eating contest, 16 cobs at a sitting and was only sick for two days! Winter, however, was a different story. As strange as it sounds, winter was the time we really missed refrigeration. Of course, if you have never had something, you have no idea you missed it.

In the fall, we would bury a winter's supply of potatoes, carrots, turnips and beets in sand in a boarded-off corner of the basement we called our root cellar. With luck, they could make it through to spring without rotting or sprouting too badly, although by the time the new crop was ready, the previous year's vegetables were almost inedible. Oh happy day, when the new potatoes arrived! They tasted like candy! Every fall, my grandmother—along with almost every other wife in the country—"put up" preserves. Back kitchens and cellars had shelves bowing under the weight of row after row of quart sealers filled with pickles, stewed tomatoes, fruits and jams.

Every once in a while, my grandfather's roving eye would spot a hen that didn't appear interested in presenting us with any more eggs, and the aroma of roast chicken would remind us of what heaven surely smelled like. We would have a goose for Christmas and our traditional rabbit for New Year's, but for pure gustatory delight, nothing challenged what we began to call "pork chop day." It was held usually around the middle of February when you wished the lights would go out so you didn't have to look at another plate of stale potatoes and salt pork.

"Pork chop day" was declared by Dad, who on a particularly miserable February day would suddenly look up from his heap of breakfast pancakes as though a ridiculous thought had just sprung into his head. Straight-faced, he would ask, "Is anyone interested in pork chops?" The response was always unanimous, instantaneous and thunderous. "Yes!" "Well, Mom," Dad would say, "better get the knife sharpened up." As farm boys, we had no mercy for the poor pig.

So there it is, staring me in the face—the Tower of Pisa, the Eiffel Tower of pork chops, just within reach of my five-year-old arm. But the pile might as well be in France because Dad is saying grace, and tonight it obviously is never going to end. This is the night when not only Hitler is dragged in, but someone named Mussolini, as well. There is concern for the King and Queen whose palace somewhere over there in England had just had a bomb dropped in its backyard. Uncle Virgil is in the bitterly cold North Atlantic with the merchant navy, which is taking a terrible pounding from something called the wolf pack.

Ravaged with guilt, I try to concentrate on the one-way conversation with God. I really do! Having heard a good deal about him, I become alarmed that what is really staring me in the nose is the devil disguised as an innocent pile of pork chops!

If you listened carefully, you knew when Dad was closing in on the end of grace. He'd slow down a bit, as though sifting through his mind to see if there was anything else worth mentioning, and while he might wander all over the map during the grace itself, he always finished with a standard sign-off: "We ask it in Christ's name—Amen."

Finally I detect the slowdown stage. The finale cannot be far-off. Listen carefully. I tense for the attack. Beneath my stockinged feet, Murphy the mutt begins to quiver.

Here it comes! Ready for the sign-off! This is it… "We ask it in Christ's name—Ame…" "PORK CHOPS." My fork slices the air in perfect synchronization with my shout. A mighty plunge into the very heart of the tower. I have my pork chop, but even as I feel the fork strike pay dirt, I sense disaster.

Imagine, if you will, the CN Tower plunging to earth: the chaos, the damage, the debris, the horror! The scattered pork chops! The flailing of tiny terrier toes on bare boards as Murphy the mutt dives for the one that hits the floor. Another embeds sail-like into the mashed potatoes.

There is a hushed silence. My arm, still fastened to my pork chop, is frozen in space. If God doesn't get me for cutting grace short, then my grandfather surely will. I await the bolt of lightening!

Although he tries not to, Uncle Ken, home for the weekend from military training at nearby Camp Borden, begins to snicker. But it is Willard, bless him, who saves the day. "Hey, Maw," he shouts, "look what I've got." Clutching a pork chop that had skittered into his lap, he lofts it high overhead, bravely waving it like a Canada Day flag.

As I have told you already, my grandmother did not have

much of a sense of humour. Tell her a joke and chances are she wouldn't get it, or if she did, wouldn't think it funny. But she loved pratfalls. Let someone slip on a banana peel and she would dissolve in tears of laughter. This is surely the pratfall of all pratfalls, and suddenly she and the entire table (except me) burst into gales of unstoppable laughter. They just can't stop. Maybe it's a kind of release from the tensions of the war. Maybe it's just cabin fever, but even Dad joins in, tears of laughter pouring down cheeks.

Orlo gets carried away a bit and starts rolling around on the floor. When we get him back up on his chair and everyone settled down, we scrape off whatever is stuck to the scattered pork chops, and as Ken always says later when telling the story, "we downed the lot with great gusto." Ken loves using words we had never heard before.

When we finish off the last battered but wonderful pork chop, Dad looks down the table at me. "Oh, oh," I think, "here it comes." He stares at me for a moment, then turns to my grandmother shaking his head. "Mom, that boy surely wants to be heard." If only he knew!

• • •

Guns and Rabbits

Somehow, by age seven, one of the more dubious skills I acquire is the ability to howl like a wolf better than a wolf, a fact duly noted by Cecil who invites me to go rabbit hunting with him. I am, of course, thrilled. Hunting with an older uncle! The Gods are surely smiling this New Year's. The fact that neither Willard nor Orlo accompany us, or ask to, would have tipped off an older or wiser boy, but I am neither.

It soon becomes apparent what hunting consists of for someone with my singular skill. Cecil takes a gentle little stroll along the well-plowed railway line, while I, bravely howling into the wind, swing out in a broad circle through waist-deep snow in dense bush. Cecil carries the shotgun with which he intends to pop any rabbit that, frightened by a mad pack of howling wolves, comes charging out of the bush across the railway track.

It is doubtful if I will ever see a rabbit; in fact, after about an hour of this I begin to doubt I will ever see my warm bed again! Looking back on it now, I consider myself fortunate that some local farmer, believing his herd was about to be set upon by Little Red Riding Hood's worst nightmare, doesn't come charging into the bush and fire off a few rounds in my direction. The young really *are* foolish!

I get my reward, though. When we finally arrive back at the house with three amazingly large jackrabbits and I flop on the floor, hoarse and exhausted, Cecil reaches down and pats my shoulder. "Good howling," he says, "really good howling." What else could you ask for? Even better, Willard and Orlo get stuck with the job of skinning and taking the guts out of the rabbits.

I didn't get a mention in Dad's New Year's dinner grace, however. God once again got all the credit, but my grandfather had a pretty good point, since it's pretty obvious God was looking out for him and his young wife when this rabbit-for-New-Year's-supper tradition began. Rabbits kept Henry and Mabel Green alive that first terrible winter spent on the Prairies. Rabbits and my grandmother's marksmanship!

We could never get Dad to come right out and say exactly what happened. From what we understand, one of the elders at the Church of God down there in Anderson, Indiana (a man named Stuckey is all we know, says my Aunt Genevieve), convinced the newly married couple that they should take their young son Gordon (my father) back to Canada. "Got a job for you," he told Henry, "up in Saskatchewan. Little place called Rouleau, just south of Regina. [Yes, the place where they film the TV show "Corner Gas."] Got a house all ready for you too. Great place to raise a family."

My grandmother was pregnant again. They needed to find a home, and "the West," just then being settled, sounded perfect. A great and bold adventure. If only they had known the truth!

In those days, the Canadian government was very anxious to establish settlements on the western prairies. By painting a wonderful picture of wide open spaces, rich harvests and thriving communities, thousands of people, many of them immigrants from Europe, were persuaded that a much better life lay just at the other end of a railway track headed west. "Go west, young man, go west," was the advertising slogan of the day. And for many it *was* a better life.

But it was hard, very hard in those early days. Even the thriving communities like Winnipeg were little more than a conglomeration of flapping tents set in mud. Every crook and con artist in the country seemed to arrive just the day before the settlers.

One of those settlers was a man named James Gray, who aptly described the scene at the railway station in Winnipeg at about the time Mom and Dad arrived in Regina. Here is Mr. Gray's account of the scene that likely confronted my grandparents as they stepped from the train:

> *In and around the railway stations were usually concentrated the greatest assemblage of pimps, pickpockets, confidence men, thugs and sneak thieves in the country. The confidence men—"boosters," they were called—concentrated on immigrants and farmers. Many of them were products of the North End slums and could speak half a dozen languages that*

enabled them to lure the immigrants into their webs. If the newcomers got past the confidence men, they had to contend with the snatch and run baggage thieves who hung around watching for something to steal. Pickpockets were such a menace that the police department had a special detail which concentrated on "dips."

Not a pretty picture. Imagine yourself, young, innocent, pregnant, and with a two-year-old crying baby, tired, dirty, hungry, dazed from endless days and nights of travel in the most primitive of conditions, in a strange city in a strange, featureless, flat land. You know not a single soul. Surrounded by chaos, dirt, noise and danger, and having very little if any money. Worst of all, your husband is not with you. You are alone with your baby, still in diapers, and another already stirring inside you.

It would only have cost a few dollars for Mabel Green's fare in what they called a "colonist coach," but one fare was all they could afford. My grandfather would have to earn his way to the great Promised Land of the West. Isabel Ecclestone Mackay wrote of people like my grandparents:

Dazzled by sun and drugged by space they wait
These homeless peoples, at our prairie gate
Dumb with the awe of those whom fate has hurled
Breathless, upon the threshold of a New World

The colonist train that brought my grandmother and two-year-old Gordon west wasn't much of an improvement over the cattle car in which her husband was riding, but at least there were no slats through which the bitter wind, rain and snow could enter. Unlike Mabel who slept on a narrow hardwood board stretched over the wooden seats, Henry could make a little nest for himself in the straw and sleep for an hour or two in relative comfort. That is until a careless cow stepped on him or, as he wryly told me once in a rare lapse into something approaching crudeness, "tried to lay a pie on me!"

My grandfather's job was to tend, clean, feed and water the trainload of cattle as it headed west. The cleaning and feeding wasn't too difficult, but having to haul enough water to satiate several dozen bawling cattle was a Herculean task if ever there was one. Each dawn and dusk, the train would shudder to a halt near a stream or lake.

Young Henry Green, with large pail in each hand, would scramble down the railway embankment, dip his pails into the cold water, clamber back up, pour them into troughs in each cattle car and repeat the process a dozen or more times. "It wasn't too bad if the water was close," he told us, "but sometimes I had to lug those pails through half a mile of bush or swamp. Cold! Cold! Cold! Well, at least there weren't any mosquitoes," he chuckled.

It was early spring, and as they rounded the north shore of Lake Superior, winter still clung tenaciously to the land. Several times Henry would have to borrow the fire axe from the train's engineer and chop a hole through the ice before the smaller ponds and lakes would surrender their precious water. When I later suggested that it seemed a tremendously difficult task for the few dollars he saved in train fare, he was genuinely astonished. "It wasn't hard work," he said. "That's just the way life was. That's what you did to survive."

What he didn't say was that the year was 1914. The ancient steam engine that hauled him westward would, in just a few days, turn about and take several hundred young men eastward to an ocean, across which lay a distant and dangerous land whose guns many would not survive.

If a picture of the house that confronted the young Green family had been used to advertise the many splendours of pioneer prairie living, the west today would still be all waving grass, roaming buffalo, prairie chickens and gophers. The house Mr. Stuckey down there in Anderson, Indiana, had enthused about, the one he claimed would be wonderful for a new family, wasn't exactly as advertised. Oh, it was a house, all right. A chicken house! Rundown, filthy, the prairie dust roaming like the buffalo in and out of the cracks in the walls.

My grandmother was so tough in her later years that she once attached a pair of pliers to an aching molar and yanked it from her own jaw, but I suspect that when she first saw that unholy mess she had a little cry…and then started to clean the place up!

My grandfather was always strangely reluctant to talk about his days in Rouleau. Almost as though he was embarrassed to have been so deceived by a man he believed to be a fellow "born again" Christian. Or more likely, he was unwilling, as he was all of his life, to criticize anyone, even a man as deceitful and evil as Mr. Stuckey. His wife wasn't as charitable. "That man," she would tell you, "was almost the death of us."

Time and retelling has blurred the portrait somewhat. My father, while writing about his family, was known to warp things a bit, "editorial licence," he called it, but as best I can paint the picture, the chicken house was a relatively minor problem. Other promises were broken. There were no supplies, and little if any equipment to work the land. I'm not even sure if he had a team of horses. Food was scarce and it is doubtful if there were neighbours within miles.

They were virtually set adrift, abandoned in a sea of waving prairie grass. I am unclear how they lived that first summer. I presume my grandfather was able to find some work, but it was my grandmother with her ability to shoot prairie chickens on the wing who fed them.

I always wondered how she could do that until many years later when I and two of my buddies found ourselves employed by a wheat farmer in Vermilion, Alberta, several hundred miles west of Rouleau.

The sight that greeted us that first crisp fall sun-up as we set out with our horse-drawn binders was something not even Disney could dream up. Whispering to us in the gentle breeze was a magnificent vast ocean of undulating golden waves. And rising from the depths of the ocean were a thousand morning suns caught in the flashing prisms of dew cascading from the wings of hundreds, no thousands of prairie chickens launching themselves into a new day.

No fences, no trees, no buildings. Golden waving wheat and golden-winged prairie chickens as far as the eye could see!

Today, sadly, most of the prairie chickens are gone, but if there were that many in 1955, can you just imagine how many there must have been in 1914? Young Mabel Green became an expert shot with the old .22 rifle, but if there were as many prairie chickens in the air as I suspect when she was out looking for supper, she could probably have tossed a rock into the air and brought down a couple!

There are no prairie chickens in winter, though. To add to the danger, my grandfather breaks a leg. My grandmother is expecting in January. With her husband not able to work and no prairie chickens to eat, how will they survive?

The answer is written in the first snowfall. Two round paw marks in front, a third back a few inches toward the middle, the fourth back another few inches and off to the side. Rabbit tracks! That is why Cecil had me out howling up a rabbit or two for what was for many years on our little Stumptown farm a traditional New Year's supper.

Rabbits were tougher targets and there weren't as many of them as there were prairie chickens. But there were enough to keep the family alive that terrible winter, a fact we celebrated each New Year's for many years.

"We had broiled rabbit, baked rabbit, roasted rabbit, fried rabbit, rabbit pie, rabbit stew and rabbit meatloaf," Mom explained once. "We could have anything we wanted to eat, so long as it was rabbit!"

She must have been one heck of a good shot. When my Aunt Genevieve was born on January 10, 1915, in that stricken little chicken house on the prairie, she weighed 10 pounds! As Genevieve told me not long ago, "Mom was either shooting a lot of rabbits, or the rabbits she shot were mighty fat!"

I want you mothers to ponder the fact that 10-pound Genevieve (who died as I finished writing this book) was born without aid of a doctor, drugs or a spinal! Not so much as an aspirin! I can hear you saying Ouch!

The little .22 rifle, without which they would surely all have perished, eventually made its way back to Arthur in the baggage of the Green family which by then numbered six. The last time I saw it, Cecil was bringing Willard up through the fields with a bullet in his leg and my grandfather was pounding the gun into splinters on a fence post.

· · ·

Daddy Is a Genius

There is a small picture on our fireplace mantel of a serious-faced little blond kid with an awful haircut, holding on for dear life to the broad back of an ancient, sleepy-looking white plow horse. You get the idea the boy doesn't entirely trust the slightly bemused-looking man into whose lap he is tucked. And if you look closely at the man, you can see the kind of smile that makes you suspect he's wondering just what kind of prank he can pull.

He's a good-looking man, aquiline nose, fine featured, slim. He can't be very tall since his legs just barely dangle beneath the horse's belly. You notice his dark hair cut short and slicked back in the fashion

of the day. He's wearing very modern-looking rimless glasses with the squared corners he preferred all his life for important occasions.

I hope he considered taking a picture with his eldest son an important occasion. I suspect those glasses were the only pair he owned, although he is sporting a nice clean white shirt and black lace-up oxfords, which means he has just arrived from the University of Michigan or is about to return. For sure, he hasn't been farming in those clothes! You really can't make out what the little kid is wearing, other than a worried look. The horse is decked out in mud, which means he has been farming.

That picture is the earliest one we have of my father and me. So far as I know, it is the only one we have of Old Bill. I look to be about two, which means my father is 26. Old Bill, in his early twenties, has been around long enough to experience more than a few shenanigans from the Green boys. You can see his ears cocked back a bit, which in horse language means "Don't be pulling any of your usual tricks, Gordon; you've got a little kid with you."

It must have been the summer of 1938. My parents weren't divorced yet, but it is in the air. My mother, like Old Bill, I guess, didn't always appreciate my father's sense of humour, or for that matter his intense love of life. Come to think of it, I'm not too sure what my mother appreciated. Certainly not me or my sister.

"You were born as part of a failed medical experiment at the University of Michigan," my father always insisted. It took me until about the age of five to catch on! The truth is, as a student my father got free medical services at the university hospital, which is a good thing since I almost died of heat prostration right in the hospital. July 7, 1936, was smack dab in the middle of the worst heat wave in Michigan history.

The day after I was born, the temperature in Detroit, only a few miles from the University of Michigan Hospital in Ann Arbor, reached 104.4 degrees Fahrenheit and for the next seven days in a row never dropped below 102 during the day. Babies, their tiny undeveloped lungs unable to cope with the tremendous heat, were dying all around me. Emergency calls went out for fans, and desperate doctors and nurses tried to cool us by blowing air over large chunks of ice. There was no air-conditioning.

All my life I had heard stories about the heat that greeted my birth, but my father was one of the country's best at spinning a yarn, so until I started writing this book, I took most of the heat-wave story with a grain of salt, or block of ice if you prefer. But lo and behold, when I started to do a bit of research, I was astonished. The truth was even more startling than my father's account. And that, believe you me, surprises the heck out of me!

Just so you don't think I am exaggerating or doing a bit of yarn spinning, let me quote just a few paragraphs from a story written July 6, 1986, by George Cantor in the *Detroit News* on the fiftieth anniversary of the heat wave.

Detroit's Killer Heat Wave of 1936
By George Cantor

When Detroiters began to die on the first day, the list was easily contained on the front page of the paper. Dora Brady, 89, in her home on Sanford. Nathan Derby, 97, in his home on West Philadelphia. A worker at Dodge Main, collapsing on the line. A man working in a laundry, another in a restaurant downtown. A night watchman found dead when the office was opened. An elderly man found in a field at Telegraph and Ann Arbor Trail. Another beneath the street sign at Burlingame and 14th.

There were 10 in all on the first day. No one could have known that it was only the beginning of one of the greatest and deadliest disasters in the history of Detroit.

Fifty years ago, the most terrible heat wave ever recorded fell upon the city. At its end, one week later, hundreds were dead and the daily lists started on the front page and filled an entire column inside the paper.

Healthy men and women would start off for work in the morning and never come home, falling in the streets or at work when they were overcome by the sun and heat. Weeping relatives besieged Receiving Hospital and the morgue where the dead were lined up in corridors since no space remained on the slabs. Doctors and nurses collapsed at their stations, overcome by heat and fatigue. "It's as if Detroit has been

*attacked by a plague out of the Middle Ages," one observer
wrote.*

*Records for high temperatures set during that summer
still stand in 15 states, including Michigan. Detroit had
counted only seven days of 100-degree readings in the 63 previous years. That mark would be equaled in the space of
seven days.*

*On Wednesday, July 8, the heat reached Detroit. By 4.50
pm the mercury registered 104.4 degrees. And the dying began.*

*The death toll took a sudden leap as news came in from
Eloise Hospital that 63 previously unreported victims had
died during the weekend. Hospitals were not air-conditioned
and heat stroke victims brought in often found no relief.
Heroic efforts were made to treat them as all rooms filled up.
Doctor and nurses, working 18 hours without a break,
administered treatment on cots or on benches in the waiting
rooms. Hysterical relatives crowded the lobby, trying to find
news of missing loved ones. Newborn infants died in the
delivery room. Old people succumbed to heat-induced heart
attacks. In a house on Magnolia, a mother and daughter died
within 12 hours of each other.*

*On the seventh day, the temperature reached 104 at
2.15 pm, July 14, then started to slide. A massive thunder-
storm swept across the city and it was over.*

It must have been those good, tough Green genes that saved me.

I once suggested to my sister that perhaps the misery my
mother must have endured during my birth is what made her so
indifferent to me. "Naw," replied Phyllis, "she didn't like me either
and I was born in November!"

It wasn't only our mother's total lack of maternal instinct that puzzled us as children. The fact that our father didn't seem to fit the fatherly mould concerned us greatly. As with all children, we would have much preferred that our father be more like the fathers we read about: busy painting the house, building something or taking us to ball games. Instead, when he wasn't off working half the night helping to build cars in Detroit, he was attending classes at Michigan or holed up for hours writing some stupid book.

"Why do you think our father is so different?" I once asked Phyllis. She looked at me like I had just fallen off the turnip truck. "Daddy is a genius," she replied disdainfully, as if everyone knew that and it explained everything. Maybe it did.

Small wonder I look so worried in that picture of us perched on Old Bill. The first memory I have of my father is him getting me to fall for a doozy, hook, line and sinker! I am about four when he gets me good for the first, but certainly not the last, time. We are on a train, bound for Ann Arbor after visiting the Greens on their Stumptown farm.

The train slows to a crawl just outside Windsor: the screech of brakes, two or three powerful jerks and a dead stop. Unlike now, in those days there is a belief that fare-paying passengers have a right to know why they are being delayed. Thus, in a few minutes a conductor comes by to inform us that one of the cars on a train ahead of us has jumped the rails and it will take an hour or so to clear the tracks so we can get on our way. I don't see the glint in my father's eye, so suspect nothing when after about half an hour he turns to me and asks if I would be all right alone for a few minutes. "I'm getting tired of waiting," he explains, "so I'm going up ahead to lift that train back on the tracks. You just sit here and don't move, I'll be back shortly."

I recall being somewhat incredulous, but this was, after all, my father assuring me it shouldn't be much of a problem. "I've done this before," he claims, "so they'll probably come looking for me soon anyway." He was gone for perhaps 10 minutes returning with shirt sleeves rolled up to his bulging biceps (well, they seemed bulging to me). "There, we should soon be on our way," he says. Then adds, "Sorry it took me so long; they didn't tell me the car was still filled with cattle. It was a bit heavier than I suspected." He leans back and feigns sleep.

Sure enough, in a few more minutes we are underway. Impressed? I guess so!

I paid him back a few months later, though. Once again we are on the train to Ann Arbor, this time after Christmas in Arthur. A few minutes out of Union Station in Toronto, the conductor comes through looking for tickets. He pauses as my father hands him his. "Half-fare if the boy is over four," says the conductor, eyeing me closely. "Oh no," my father lies straight-faced. "He's not four 'til next month." My protest is immediate and loud: "My birthday is July 7 and I'm four and a half." Laughter ripples through the coach. Red-faced, my father pays up.

Most of my father's jokes were harmless enough. Winding almost invisible fine wire from a Model T coil around Cecil's bed-posts, so when he sneaks in from late-night courting and tries to jump silently into bed he bounces back off the wire with a yell loud enough to wake the dead would be a typical prank.

One joke, however, almost lands him in jail. It is after the war, and my father is one of the editors of the *Family Herald and Weekly Star*, the bible of rural Canada. Our small farm north of Montreal provides an abundance of very large goose eggs. My father and fellow conspirator and editor Vernon Pope discover the eggs make a wonderful splash when dropped from an open window onto the tops of vans as they whip along St. James Street, three floors below. Timing is crucial. Correctly gauge the vehicle's speed, watch for unsuspecting pedestrians, give the egg just the right degree of thrust out the window, and the results can be quite spectacular!

You've got to understand that this occurred long before the separatist threats in Quebec, when Montreal's St. James Street was the heart of Canada's financial district. Very much like Bay Street in Toronto is today. As a consequence, there were only two kinds of vehicles using the street: those belonging to the very rich and important, and the trucks and vans that supplied the banks and other financial institutions which kept the rich rich and the important important. There was no great problem if a wayward goose egg missed the roof and struck the windshield or hood of a truck or van. Working men didn't have the time to go on a wild goose-egg chase! The rich, on the other hand, have working men to do the chasing for them.

Thus, when the inevitable occurs and an egg smacks a limousine's windshield dead centre, all hell breaks loose. Before you know it, the street and then the offices of both the *Family Herald* and the *Montreal Star* that share the building are filled with police.

Had it not been for the fact that he was notorious throughout the *Family Herald* and the *Montreal Star* for his pranks and that office bets were being placed on the accuracy of his bombing raids, I am sure my father would have tried bluffing it out. Knowing full well someone would soon blow the whistle on him, he bravely steps forward and confesses. Besides which, his desk is full of goose eggs, and police are checking every drawer in the building.

The very excitable and much offended recipient of the goose-egged window is some big shot with the nearby Bank of Montreal head office. Were it not for the intervention of my father's good friend Frank Selke, there's every chance he would have spent a few days in one of Montreal's danker jails. But in those days it was pretty hard for the Montreal police or a bank official to ignore an appeal from the General Manager of the Stanley Cup Champion Montreal Canadiens.

"Gordon," instructs Mr. Selke in that quiet but no-nonsense voice of his, "I think you should be putting your goose eggs some-place other than on the windshields of St. James Street cars. They tell me they won't lay charges this time, but if you ever try it again, I doubt whether even a call from Rocket Richard will dissuade them from lowering the boom on you." That was the end of that!

Interestingly, it wasn't long after that incident that we had to rescue that same Frank Selke from the wrath of the Westmount police.

We got the plea for help before dawn one Saturday morning. I took the phone call. Frank Selke was about the calmest, coolest, most collected person you would ever meet, but he sounded about as rattled as I suspect he could ever be. "Lowell, is that you?" He is whispering and I can barely hear him. Without waiting for my reply, he fires off instructions. "The police are only a couple of blocks away, how soon can you get here?"

By this time my father has shaken himself from bed, and realizing who was on the other end of the line, he becomes alarmed. The instructions continue. "Come right into the garage, I'll have the door open for you. We haven't got much time." He mutters something, then hangs up.

When the General Manager of the Montreal Canadiens tells you to get your buns to his place pronto, believe you me you do not argue! We have an old Buick Roadmaster which, having seen far too much road, is known to oppose early morning wake-ups. Sensing the urgency, this time it co-operates beautifully and fires up at the first turn of the key.

It is a good 45 minutes from our little farm on Côte St. Francois, St. Maurice en Haut, Bois des Fillion, Ste-Thérèse-de-Blainville

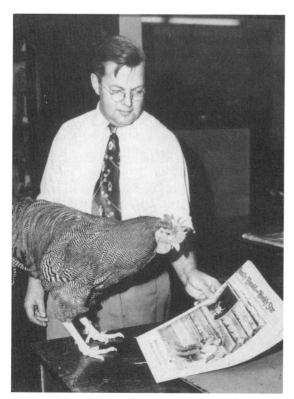

One of H. Gordon Green's champion Barred Rock roosters give the "peck of approval" to another edition of the *Family Herald and Weekly Star*, the most read magazine in Canada while Gordon was editor. Gordon would often bring farm animals into the office on Montreal's St. James Street. This included calves, lambs, and on one occasion, a pig. "Just to remind everyone what a farm animal looks and smells like," he claimed!

(our mailing address!) to Frank Selke's palatial home on Upper Westmount Boulevard, or simply "The Boulevard" as everyone still calls it. Upper Westmount Boulevard, I will have you know, was and still is just about the ritziest street in Canada. Mr. Selke's home was only a couple of blocks from the house Pierre Trudeau bought many years later. But despite the obvious demands for decorum such a prestigious address requires, it doesn't stop Mr. Selke from raising his world-famous Golden Pencilled Hamburg chickens in his garage.

Fairly handy with a saw and a hammer, Mr. Selke had very cleverly tacked a false front onto his garage and installed a little nursery for his beloved exotic chickens whose parents win him prizes all throughout North America. This works fine until one morning a couple of them, awaking to the primal stirrings of avian testosterone, suddenly discover that they are roosters and began to act accordingly. Which is to say they begin to crow like crazy.

Faced with what is a clear and present danger, an ominous threat to the peace and security of Westmount, several properly outraged residents call police. "Good God, someone is raising chickens in Westmount!" A more heinous crime could scarcely be imagined!

That old Buick is a credit to her maker. For a change, all eight pistons pound in perfect harmony, not a hiccup as we roar up the north slope of Mount Royal and soar down to The Boulevard. Sharp left through an open garage door and we're there, just a few houses ahead of police search parties that are going house to house in a massive chicken hunt. The garage door descends behind us, and there stands Mr. Selke, four chickens dangling by their legs from his hands.

Then it hits me! That mumble on the phone meant "bring cages." In our haste, we had forgotten to bring anything in which to store the chickens on their dash to safety. Mr. Selke shakes his head in disbelief. "You didn't bring cages?!" But the man who deals on a daily basis with the likes of Rocket Richard, Doug Harvey and Toe Blake knows how to take control of a delicate situation. Giving our old Buick a brief appraising glance, "open a back window," he orders. He drops the four dangling birds onto the back seat, followed in quick succession by the remaining dozen or so.

The garage door slides open, Mr. Selke sticks his head out and gives a furtive glance up and down The Boulevard. "Go," he growls. And we are off!

For a moment or two, the chickens are cowed by their sudden change of venue and, no doubt, the opulence of a Buick's back seat. They remain crouched out of sight as we nonchalantly motor past two Westmount patrol cars now parked only two houses from the Selke garage. As we turn north and head for the safety of Côte St. Francois, all hell breaks loose! As if at a given signal, every Golden Pencilled Hamburg adolescent makes a break for it.

You have doubtless heard the expression, "running around like a chicken with its head cut off." Well, let me tell you, a chicken with its head still on is not a heck of a lot smarter than one with its head removed.

There are chickens flying into everything, including my head and the front windshield. My father is laughing so hard he's useless at protecting my sight lines. I'm laughing, swatting chickens away from my face and yelling, "Get them off me—I can't see to drive."

By the time we pull into our driveway, the chickens have pretty well pooped themselves out in more ways than one. Safely stowed in our little chicken house, they immediately begin to innocently peck away at the floor as though nothing has happened. Then I spot it. A giant white bird turd streaks down my father's glasses and splashes his shirt. We are so convulsed with laughter that Daisy the bulldog rouses herself from her perpetual state of semi-hibernation and tears out to see what's up.

The years we were kept apart magnifies the joy my father and I share this day.

. . .

Of Chickens, Hockey and Feed Pails

There is no joy when next we are summoned to rescue chickens from Westmount. Once again it is Frank Selke who makes the call. This time to my father. The instructions are definitive: "No one is to know what's going on. You can't tell a soul what's happening. If word gets out now, it will be hell on wheels!"

Thus, sworn to secrecy, we regretfully spend a sunny fall day in 1955 on the slopes of Mount Royal, catching Dick Irvin's beloved world champion exotic chickens. Proudly strutting Golden Pencilled Hamburgs, broad-breasted Buff Orphingtons, Silkies with their rabbit fur feathers, Polish whose crazy floppy feather hats so cover their eyes they are prone to walking into walls, and at least a dozen other breeds. Winners of many a poultry show.

Their little fenced-in runs, each with a tiny roosting hut, are helter-skeltered over half an acre of mountainside grass. Everyone knows they are there, but unlike the mansion owners near Frank Selke, no one seems to mind the early-morning crowing. Besides, these chickens belong to the man who took over the reins of a sad-sack Montreal Canadiens hockey team in 1940 and turned it into a powerhouse. The man who brought three Stanley Cups to Montreal. Dick Irvin, the wily "Silver Fox." The man who discovered Rocket Richard and created the "Punch Line"—Maurice Richard, Toe Blake and Elmer Lach—perhaps the greatest line in hockey history. Dick Irvin, the man who raised his chickens on the slopes of Mount Royal!

What we and only a handful of people in the country know that afternoon is that a bombshell is about to be dropped. After 15 years, Dick Irvin is leaving Montreal. Going to Chicago to coach the Black Hawks.

Frank Selke told me later it was one of the most difficult decisions of his life, but he blamed Dick Irvin, at least in part, for the terrible riot that rocked Montreal just prior to the 1955 playoffs. Fans went on a rampage when Rocket Richard was suspended just prior to the Stanley Cup finals with Detroit. Frank felt that Dick Irvin had goaded Richard to the point where an "explosion" on the ice was almost inevitable.

The incident in which Richard attacked a linesman and was suspended for the final three games of the season and the playoffs

Frank J. Selke, general manager of the Montreal Canadiens,
Gordon Green and a champion Golden Pencilled Hamburg

cost the team the league championship and the Stanley Cup,
claimed Selke. It also cost Richard the scoring championship.
Frank Selke told Dick Irvin he could stay with the Canadiens but
he couldn't coach them. Irvin left to coach Chicago, but was only
able to do so for part of the following season. He died an untimely
death in 1957, victim of a rare form of bone cancer.

In his book *Behind the Cheering* which he wrote with my
father, Frank Selke revealed for the first time that earlier in the
season, prior to a game against Toronto, Dick Irvin told Maple
Leaf General Manager Con Smythe that if Chicago offered him
enough money he'd coach them. When Frank Selke confronted
Dick with this, Irvin brushed it off, but you certainly get the idea
that Selke was more than a little miffed that his good friend would
go behind his back in this manner.

My father claimed he knew nothing more about it than what

Frank told both of us. I am not even sure if Dick Irvin Jr. of "Hockey Night in Canada" fame knows the full story.

Nor do I recall what happened to those prize chickens of Dick Irvin's that we rounded up that afternoon on Mount Royal. What I do remember is that Frank Selke was a sad man for a long time. Dick Irvin had been a very close friend, sharing not only a love of hockey and the Canadiens, but the chicken fancy as well.

One of the lesser-known stories of the NHL is the manner in which for about 10 years the league-playing schedule was formulated to accommodate the exotic chicken hobbies of Frank Selke and Dick Irvin. With only a six-team league, it wasn't that difficult. All that was required was that the Montreal Canadiens play the Toronto Maple Leafs in Toronto while the Royal Winter Fair was on.

The Royal Winter Fair was, and still is, one of the largest agricultural fairs in the world. Farmers from across Canada and some from the United States bring their prize cattle, sheep, hogs, horses and chickens to be shown and judged. Even a third prize from "The Royal" brings fame—and in some cases no small fortune—to the owner. There isn't much of a fortune to be made from showing chickens, but in the small world of the "chicken fancy," fame is far more important.

Thus it was that every year during The Royal, two of the most powerful and famous men in the world of hockey would follow the poultry judges around from cage to cage, agonizing and rejoicing just as much over victory and defeat of their chickens as they would that night over the game against the Leafs.

As he was apt to do in times of stress, Mr. Selke spent a good deal of time at our farm. It was an escape from the whirlwind swirling about the Irvin departure. He arrived each morning with a truckload of scrap wood and filled the day with hammering and sawing.

Each day our little chicken house grew longer and longer, not necessarily always in exactly the same direction. Some days it wandering off a bit to the west, sometimes to the east. It zigged when it should have zagged, zagged when it should have zigged. In places it sagged. Frank Selke, a licensed electrician by trade, was handy enough with a hammer and saw, but was somewhat hazy on the concepts of "level" and "straight." I doubt he even owned a measuring tape. Trying to open or close doors between the various individual compartments was often an adventure. An intrigued visitor once asked what school of architecture Mr. Selke subscribed to. "Whimsical," replied my father.

The chickens didn't seem to mind. Each breed had its own separate compartment. Each rooster had his own little harem. Feeding and cleaning, on the other hand, was a nightmare. That was my job the year I lived there on Côte St. Francois, St. Maurice en Haunt, Bois des Fillion, Ste-Thérèse-de-Blainville.

If you squinted your eyes a bit and used your imagination, the chicken house, as it crept further and further into the distance, began to resemble a train wreck, cars heading off in all directions. It looked even stranger inside! Most of Frank Selke's building materials came from the Forum. It was amazing what the various shows and functions left behind when they moved on.

One of the largest sections had walls constructed entirely from plywood models of lions, tigers and elephants. The roof featured about three-quarters of a huge, garishly painted clown's face. Part of a sign with the letters "ling Bros, Barnum and Bailey Cir" completed the masterpiece. In deference to its magnificence, that room was thereafter known as the Sistine Chapel, later shortened to just "the chapel," as in "let's put the Rhode Island Reds (a breed of chicken) in the third section past the chapel."

One day, Mr. Selke showed up with a dump truck grunting beneath the weight of an immense pile of white boards, which upon close inspection looked like an army had attacked with bayonets and black markers. Mr. Selke summoned me over. "Have a look here. See this?" He pointed to a large black smudge, stark against the white. "That's the Rocket!"

Each year all the boards surrounding the Forum rink are replaced, and that year the old ones, complete with skate marks and puck skids, were going to advance our train wreck of a chicken house a few feet further along the tracks! Whether that particular puck mark was indeed from a Rocket Richard shot, I'm sure Frank Selke had no way of knowing. I chose to believe him. Some of those marks surely were the Rocket's!

One of the things we always needed more of as our chicken brood grew was pails for feed and water. As luck would have it, the *Montreal Star* offices, just below those of the *Family Herald*, were getting new floors—the old tile ripped out and new installed. In those days, rather than attached to each tile, the glue came in large pails which, when emptied, were perfect for feed and water buckets. My father had a standing order for these pails with the tile installers. Each day for a couple of weeks, he lugged one or two of these pails home, feeling very proud of himself. No one else wanted the pails because it was impossible to scrape them clean of the glue that remained.

It didn't take my father long to figure out the solution. He took a pail outside, dropped a lighted match into it and the problem was solved. The glue burned fiercely. "Cauterized her," said my father. "As squeaky clean as a politician on election day!" It became a ritual. Each night upon returning home with his prize pail, my father hiked to the backyard, dropped a match and watched the pail burn. "Other guys kick the bucket," he said, "I burn pails!"

They had just finished the tile job the day my friend Mike Phillips and I joined my father for the bus trip home to Côte St.

Francois. We planned on doing a bit of target shooting and maybe some fishing the next day, so we'd spent the day in Montreal ogling the girls and picking up some fishing line and .22 bullets. Mike was the kind of guy who always wanted to help, so it was only natural that he offered to carry home that last glue pail. As usual, my father took the pail when we got home, and as Mike and I sat down with the rest of the family for dinner, we watched through the window as the pail-lighting ritual began.

Suddenly all hell broke loose! Machine-gun fire in the backyard! The pail began a crazy dance. My father screamed and ran. Fortunately, he wasn't far from cement steps that descended into our cellar. They may have saved his life. He dove head first down the steps and lay huddled. "Military training," he told us later.

Those of us around the dinner table were momentarily frozen with shock. "The bullets," screamed Mike and dove under the table. By this time the gunfire had stopped. All was quiet on the Côte St. Francois front! The pail lay on its side, a few desultory flames flickered through its riddled sides. My father poked his head cautiously up from his cement bunker and looked around. Mike emerged from under the table.

Believe it or not, one of the bullets had actually gone through a crease in my father's pants, but hadn't scratched his skin. We found several holes in the side of the house where bullets had buried themselves. Several more peppered the chicken house.

What had happened was that Mike had dropped the fishing line, the bullets and a couple of bags of groceries into the pail as we swung along St. James Street to the bus. When he got home, my father took the pail and dumped what he thought was everything onto the ground. The package of .22 shells, however, stuck to the glue on the bottom of the pail. When he dropped the match, well, you know what happened!

We laughed about it for years. Mike still tells the story to anyone who will listen, but to tell the truth it wasn't all that funny when it happened. My father tried to sell the story to *Reader's Digest*, but I suspect they thought it was just too crazy to be believed. It was one of the few times they turned him down. Maybe it was the headline he suggested: "How I Almost Shot Myself With a Feed Pail!"

* * *

Guns and Groundhogs

If I were to buy any of my grandchildren a set of toy guns, their mothers would likely have me brought up on charges. I'm not sure you can even buy the kind of toy guns—with their splendid decorated holsters—we used to strap low on our hips. Guns, even the toy kind, are not politically correct these days, but when I was a boy, even little girls played with them.

Eaton's Catalogue showed up at our front door one Christmas with a front-page picture of a beautiful little blond-haired girl dazzling in a Dale Evans "deluxe edition" cowgirl outfit, complete with twin silver-barrelled, bone-handled cap pistols encased in bright gold and silver holsters. "Personally endorsed by Dale Evans herself," read the ad. "Authentic right down to the calfskin vest and the pure leather cowgirl boots. Your little cowgirl will be thrilled this Christmas."

Of course, I wouldn't have been caught dead anywhere near anything to do with Dale Evans. We boys didn't mind Roy Rogers, but we booed the movie screen every time Dale showed up. Mainly because that's when Roy would stop shooting the bad guys and start singing.

My hero was Hopalong Cassidy. He didn't do any singing and his guns were stowed in delightfully deadly looking black holsters. I got lucky one summer and won enough marbles to trade them for a considerably used Hopalong Cassidy gun and holster set. The hammers on both guns were broken, which meant you couldn't fire caps with them. That didn't matter much because I couldn't really afford caps anyway. They were just fine for playing cowboys and Indians, and if we couldn't persuade anyone to be an Indian, good guys and bad guys was almost as much fun. There is never a problem finding boys quite willing to play "bad guys."

My grandchildren will doubtless be shocked to learn that when I was growing up we all played a game called "cowboys and Indians." It would not be allowed or even dreamed of today, especially when, as you have probably suspected, the cowboys were the good guys. The Indians, well let's just say they were not the good guys. Mind you, that was the way it was generally presented to us in the movies and in the books we read. The idea that the Indians were the good guys being exploited by the bad cowboys is a relatively new concept.

No Roy Rogers, no Hopalong Cassidy, no toy guns and no cowboys and Indians! No wonder so many kids today seem totally bored. How we would have survived growing up without them, I have no idea.

Has any of the new, politically correct method of raising children improved children's play? Has any of this improved parenting improved children generally? To tell the truth, I think kids, with their guns, their cowboys and Indians and their political incorrectness, were just as good when I was a boy as they are today. If really pressed on the matter, I would have to say I think we had more fun.

The toy guns quickly progressed into the real thing. Most children growing up on farms in the years during and immediately following WWII started using .22 rifles and even shotguns at a very early age. There's a picture of me in our scrapbook, about ten years of age, aiming a rifle at something. The gun appears to be about as big as I am.

I don't recall ever getting any instructions on the proper use of guns, other than my grandfather very gravely telling us to "never, ever point a gun at anything we did not intend to kill."

Having used guns to shoot groundhogs and sometimes foxes raiding our chicken houses, we understood the destructive power of the weapon only too well. We played with our toy guns, but we knew enough not to play around with real ones. Maybe it was because we were expected to act mature and responsible that the thought of doing otherwise never entered our heads. At least not with anything as serious as a gun.

But as we all learned one afternoon, accidents do happen, even to careful and responsible boys.

Willard, Orlo and I had spent the afternoon stalking a couple of wily old groundhogs burrowed deep into the banks of the little stream that ran along the back of our Stumptown farm. Our gun was the .22 Mom had shot prairie chickens and rabbits with back in Saskatchewan to keep the family alive, which meant it was at least 30 years old and probably older. We kept it as polished up as we could, but it was beginning to fall apart and had a hair-trigger. Dad never really forgave himself for what happened. "I should have smashed that thing years ago," he said later.

Orlo had the gun. He was holding it properly, pointed to the ground. Willard was just ahead; I trailed behind. Willard jumped across a narrow ditch. Orlo followed, raising the gun just slightly during the leap. At that instant, the gun went off and Willard fell to the ground screaming.

The bullet entered his right leg just above the heel.

Looking back on it now, I am amazed at how three young boys reacted so quickly and calmly. Dropping to his knees, Orlo ripped off his shirt and tied it tightly around Willard's leg, which was bleeding profusely. Without a word being said, it was immediately understood that Orlo would stay with Willard while I ran for help.

It was close to a mile back to our farmhouse. Several fences had to be climbed. I was breathless when I plunged into the kitchen. "Willard's been shot!" Mom went white and clutched the table for support. "In the leg," I managed to gasp.

The rest of it is a kind of blur. I suppose I was in some kind of shock coupled with exhaustion from the frantic run. Dad and Cecil harnessed the team of horses to a wagon, and instead of taking the long away around by the road, they took the most direct route through the fields, cutting gaps in the fences as they went.

The Village of Arthur had only one doctor at the time. A man well-known for being in his cups most of the day. Which is a polite way of saying he drank a lot. "Why would a sober man want to doctor in a place like Arthur?" asked my Uncle Virgil once.

When the doctor showed up at our farm prepared to extract the bullet, he was weaving more than a little and you could smell the booze the moment he entered our driveway. Mabel Green took one look and one whiff and booted him out the door. Not quite literally, but almost. "You've been drinking. Don't come near that boy!"

Thus it was that, so far as I know, Willard became the first member of the Henry Green family to ever see the inside of a hospital. They did a great job up there in Fergus. Even gave Willard the battered old slug they removed from his ankle. He kept it for years as a kind of badge of honour.

What I didn't know at the time was that years would pass before the three of us would hunt groundhogs again or do anything else together on that little farm. My world was about to be shattered.

• • •

Kidnapped!

The first indication of trouble came while I slept. According to Orlo who watched it all through a crack in the floorboards (our secret "spy hole" to the kitchen below), I missed a lot of excitement. "You should have seen Dad," he breathlessly told me the next morning. "He had that Mr. Wainman backed right up against the wall and told him he couldn't have you and Phyllis."

If what Orlo told me the next morning is true, and to this day he swears it is, it must indeed have been something to see. David Wainman was a good head taller than Henry Green who, thanks to decades of his wife's pies, tended to be on the slightly rotund side. David was tall and spare, as tough as nails, and having spent a winter in a lumber camp had probably been involved in more than a few scraps. Henry Green, on the other hand, had not likely ever raised a hand in anger against another man.

A grandfather standoff in our little Stumptown kitchen!

In the end, it was David who backed down and slunk out of the house empty-handed. "Lowell and Phyllis are staying right where they are. Right here," Dad said. "They are not going with you and that's that!"

Sadly, he underestimated my mother's cunning determination.

My maternal grandfather David Wainman, that is my mother's father, was not a bad man. He was a weak man. Easily led, especially by women. My mother was a manipulative, mean-spirited, rigid woman who was only too willing to lead him where he should not have gone.

For a number of years, David Wainman farmed only a few miles from where Henry Green was raising his ever-expanding brood. It was during that time that my mother, Joan Wainman, and my father, Gordon Green, met at the Arthur High School. They dated despite the vociferous objections of Joan's father. David Wainman hated Gordon Green. It's not surprising.

My father was a cocky little guy. "Strutted around like a peacock," I overheard Grandfather Wainman say. Even then, my father had aspirations to be either a writer or musician. He'd launched a little business called the Gordon Green Concert Company. He and several other high school students travelled the area starring in musical and drama concerts written and directed by my father. I have a little booklet that has survived the years, entitled "Green's Humorous Dialogues." It contains five of what are described as playlets and one full-blown play entitled "The April Fool." The writing shows great promise.

Grandfather Wainman would not have understood any of that. He would view the man dating his daughter as a fast-talking, smart aleck who would never do an honest day's work in his life. The fact he was a Green didn't help much either.

My father used to tell the story of him calling on Joan and being confronted by her father. David was about to throw a set of harness over a mare's back, but instead hurled it into the barn gutter. "You, Gordon, get out of here," shouted David, "and take that bulldog bitch with you." If, in fact, my grandfather actually used language that strong, he must have been very irate indeed. The closest I ever heard him come to actual swearing was the time a horse kicked him square in the chest, dropping him with a grunt onto the concrete floor. When he caught his breath, "darn!" was all he said.

As with almost everything else in his life, David had only marginal success farming in Arthur. When his wife Nettie died, he sold out and moved to an even poorer farm just north of Orillia, where he once again scratched out a meagre living and married a dried-up religious fanatic of a woman named Lila Byers.

Joan Wainman married Gordon Green despite, or maybe because of, the objections of her father. They moved into a cramped, decrepit house trailer in Ann Arbor, Michigan, while my father attended the University of Michigan. To support us, my father worked at various jobs during the night, then attended classes during the day.

When they divorced, a judge ruled that Phyllis and I should live with our paternal grandparents Henry and Mabel Green in Arthur. It was a wise decision. We were happy and much loved in that little Stumptown farmhouse. Sadly, it was not to last.

• • •

For the life of me, I can't remember the name of the grades one and two teacher who, with a broad smile, said that my mother had come to visit Phyllis and me and it was okay if we left class for a few minutes. I remember liking that teacher because she let me help the grade ones with their reading. This included my sister Phyllis who, along with the rest of the grade ones, sat in the same room with those of us in grade two. I had already mastered *Dick and Jane* and felt pretty proud of myself when allowed to stroll across the room to help the grade ones who were struggling mightily with words like "Spot" and "see."

I am certain the teacher had no idea she was being used to facilitate a kidnapping. If Willard, or even Orlo, had been in the same classroom, I am certain they would have sounded the alarm, but the higher grades were in another room. I was too young and far too innocent to even contemplate the perfidiousness some adults are capable of. When my mother ordered us into Grandpa

Wainman's old Hudson Super Six, idling in front of the school, I dutifully obeyed, never suspecting the disaster that was befalling us. It was only when my mother told us to lie on the floor so no one could see us that warning lights began to light up.

I didn't cry as Polly and Charlie followed us to the edge of town; I was probably too afraid of my mother. But as we pulled away from the familiar streets of Arthur and the crows gave up their chase, something very strange happened to me. My mind refused to record what was happening. Try as I might, I cannot recall a single thing of that trip from Arthur to Orillia after the crows disappeared. I remember, very vividly, the smiling teacher telling us our mother was here for a visit. Getting into the car and lying on the floor seems like only yesterday. I can still see Polly and Charlie's curious silent swooping…but the rest of it is a total blank. I can recall nothing until the following morning when a new class-mate demanded a rigorous test of the new kid in the schoolyard.

Whitey Green was his name. We could have been twins. We were the same age, same last name, same size, same blond hair, and we were both new at that little one-room schoolhouse about 15 miles north of Orillia. It seemed only natural to the incumbents that *Lowell* Green, who had arrived only that morning, should fight recently arrived tough guy *Whitey* Green. Welcome to Lake St. George Public School, 12th Concession, Orillia Township, October, 1943.

I could tell that Whitey didn't really want to fight. He'd pulled the mantle of "tough guy" over himself to mask the anger and shame of a knockabout life and a drunk for a father. His family had moved into a tottery old farmhouse just up the road from the school only a couple of weeks before I arrived. If history was any judge, they'd probably soon be moving on again when the rent came up short.

The students had Whitey Green pretty well figured out by the morning of my arrival, but I was an enigma just landed in the schoolyard with no explanation and no warning. For all they knew, I had just arrived from Mars. A test was mandatory!

And so Whitey Green and Lowell Green, looking for all the world like brothers, but in actual fact no relation, went at it there just inside the front gate of Lake St. George School. We didn't want to fight, but knew there was no escape. We rolled around on the ground a few times, threw a few punches, and the spectators cheered us on. Then, at word the teacher was arriving, they picked us up off the ground, helped to dust us off, and together all we good buddies welcomed the teacher and went to class!

• • •

Phyllis and Lowell in Orillia shortly after the abduction. We were not happy campers!

The Mailbox

The mailbox became my beacon of hope. This is where word from the outside world, maybe even news of rescue, would arrive. Or so I believed.

It was a mailbox like any other you'll see in rural areas today. Galvanized metal affixed to a solid wooden post. "David Wainman" painted in black letters on both sides. Unlike most in use today, it swivelled on the post. Facing the road meant mail had arrived; parallel to the road signalled empty.

It was exactly one mile from my new home on the 11th Concession of Orillia Township to Lake St. George Public School on the 12th Concession. Through farmers' fields, over fences, through bush and across a stream. (Today the fields are the well-groomed Lake St. George Golf and Country Club.) It was a slow and usually solitary walk to school each morning, but there was no dawdling on the way home. The teacher had a little hand-held bell, which she rang to dismiss all eight grades each afternoon at four o'clock. At the first sweet ding, I was out of my seat for a one-mile dash. I ran that mile home certain that today would be the day. There would be a letter.

But no amount of wishing could get that mailbox to face the road. I tried prayer. "Dear God, please let there be a letter for me this time. I'm sorry for all the bad things I've done. I promise never to do them again." And promises even more fantastic than that were made if only God would put a letter for me in that mailbox.

Why I never suspected that any mail would long ago have been retrieved by others, I do not know. I was absolutely convinced that if I saw the mailbox turned to face the road when I crested that final hill before home it meant a letter from my father.

Sometimes my eyes, or more likely my mind, played tricks on me. With little effort I could convince myself that this time the mailbox was turned. Only by actually opening the lid and peering inside could I force myself to accept the truth. No one cared enough to write. Not even my father. Or so I was allowed to believe!

Phyllis had only to cross a road to get to her school. Not our road. Not the 11th Concession but another road miles the other side of Orillia. It might as well have been on the other side of the moon! Not only had my mother and grandfather snatched us from the large and loving Green family, they tore brother and sister apart.

My mother always claimed the only reason she married my father was to escape from her father's new wife, Lila, whom we were instructed to call Aunt Lila. Yet it was into that home that she sentenced me. Phyllis was shipped off to live with Aunt Lila's unmarried sister, Florence Byers, and her father (known to us all as simply Old Man Byers), a mostly blind, doddering old man who ruled the family like some kind of ancient potentate. Just to complete the household was Lily, old man Byers' elderly, widowed sister. As you can imagine, it was a less-than-perfect place for a six-year-old girl to be planted into.

Phyllis was never allowed to have friends to their house, apparently in fear they might scuff some paint or, heaven forbid, eat some of the Byers' provisions. Phyllis did manage once to get a little girl to come and play with her with a promise that they could have an apple, of which they had a basement full. No such luck; Lily stood guard at the top of the cellar steps to insure that no little girl got her grubby hands on one of their apples. One of Old Man Byers' rules was that there was to be no eating between meals. Another was that you were not allowed to argue.

Grandpa Wainman had no love for Old Man Byers, primarily

because the old man refused to die. I suspect the main reason my grandfather married Lila was in the belief that her elderly father would soon kick off, leaving some of his considerable wealth to Lila and thus to him. Old Man Byers, being no fool, must have been aware of this, and I am certain it was out of pure spite that he refused to die before his son-in-law

I need not go into more detail—I am sure by now you get the picture. We had not exactly been transported to paradise!

It might have been more understandable if we had gone to live with our mother, but incredibly, after ordering us to lie on the floor of the "escape" car, our mother essentially disappeared from our lives for the next two years. I was astonished years later when she complained to me that the kidnapping forced her to miss two days of work from her job with the Wartime Prices and Trades Board in Ottawa. Mind you, she didn't call it kidnapping. Until the day she died, she maintained that she rescued us. From what she never made clear.

Was it all for money? My father always insisted that was the sole reason. The US Army was paying $10 per month per child to guardians. In a day when you could buy an entire farm for four or five thousand dollars, and huge cabbages sold for five cents, that was a lot of money! For that scheming, mercenary rogues' gallery, it was perfect: kick my father when he couldn't fight back and make some money in the process.

To top it all off, they all believed themselves so holy that ordinary churches wouldn't do. The church I was compelled to attend was one of those without a minister. Various members of the congregation, the born agains, got up and delivered little homilies, lectures and testimonials usually intended to scare the bejabbers out of us poor beggars sitting in the back rows.

You sat in the back row until you "answered the call" and

became "saved." There was my grandfather and Lila, along with other family members—"God's chosen people"—in the front pews, fresh from kidnapping and breaking hearts, while Phyllis and I were relegated to the rear.

For awhile Pastor Guthrie, the charismatic minister at Orillia's Bethel Baptist Church, persuaded Aunt Lila to switch venues. My grandfather agreed, perhaps relieved that he no longer had to "stand and deliver" at their old church.

That honeymoon ended when the charismatic pastor and a member of the choir disappeared one day with a considerable pile of parishioners' money. This was the guy whose graphic descriptions of hell gave me nightmares. Instead of just talking about eternal damnation, he had the knack of describing hellish horrors in everyday terms that even a kid like me could easily understand and relate to.

"Did you ever scald yourself?" he asked in one particularly picturesque sermon. "Accidentally spill boiling water on your hand? Remember the terrible pain? Remember how you couldn't stand it? Hell is just like that, except," here he paused for effect, "except, you are buried to your neck in boiling water and you never get out!" It almost scared me enough to send me scurrying up to the front to get "saved" and baptized, but not quite.

Come to think of it, the mental image of our charismatic "preacher friend" soaking in boiling water for eternity is somewhat attractive. I can even think of a few other people I wouldn't mind him sharing the "bath" with!

The terrible silence of the mailbox continued for more than a year. Nothing was heard of, or from, the Greens. It was as if the entire family had been wiped from the face of the earth. I dared not even mention their names. We were learning about magnetic polarity at school, and I began to imagine that a giant magnetic field swirled around me constantly, repelling those attempting to reach me.

Little did I know how close my imagination was to reality!

It was actually more than a year before I heard anything of my father. I had come to believe he was probably dead. Out of the blue one day, as we were milking the cows during evening chores, my grandfather said, "Looks like your father is going to the Philippines." I feigned minor interest. "Where's that?" "The South Seas, near Australia," he said.

I was intrigued to hear him even mention my father's name, but the Philippines meant nothing to me. I had no idea why my father would go there. The huge Lipton's Tea map we used at school to follow the progress of the war showed only Europe. We knew that finally the good guys—us—were winning, but in grade three we knew nothing of the war in the Pacific.

My mother was visiting at the time, on special leave from the government, she said, because of her nerves. Over dinner I foolishly asked her if she knew anything about the Philippines. Her head snapped around. "Why do you ask me that?" Without thinking I answered, "Well, Grandpa says my Dad is going there." She turned on her father with anger. "Why would you tell him that? Why would you tell him that his father is going into one of the worst war zones in the world?" Grandpa Wainman had no response.

The bottom of my stomach fell out! They were going to send my father off to be killed. I would never see him again! There wasn't a soul I could convey my fears to. As I look back now, it is perhaps the cruelest thing my mother ever did, and my grandfather must have known it and was sorry for the role he had played.

That night he crept into the dark of my bedroom. I couldn't see his face, but his breathing sounded strange. Was he crying? I cannot say. He leaned over the bed and softly whispered something I treasure to this day: "Grandpa loves ya." I said nothing but forgave him all.

As I was about to learn, there was certainly plenty to forgive. It was a few weeks after the Philippines episode that I finally heard from my father.

I cannot recall the name of the teacher who taught those eight grades at Lake St. George Public School in 1944. It must have been very difficult. Some of the boys in grade eight were probably only a couple of years younger than she because in those days you could actually fail a grade and sometimes two! I remember we all liked her and she was a good baseball player who joined in during our noon-hour and recess games. She must have been very brave, as well.

"Lowell," she said one day, "could you please stay after school for a few minutes, I have something I want to go over with you." I hadn't done anything deserving of detention so was only slightly apprehensive. "Come up to the front," she said after everyone had left. "I have a letter here from your father."

I don't remember much of what was in that letter, other than he had been trying to get in touch with me from the first day we were snatched from the Arthur school. He had written, he said, dozens of letters but they had all been returned unopened. He said everyone in Arthur missed Phyllis and I terribly and that even Polly and Charlie seemed depressed. He wanted to know if I enjoyed my new school and I remember assuring the teacher that I did. Best of all, he said that I would soon start getting letters and even presents in the mail from him. It was the happiest day of my life.

There was hell to pay later, though. John Hawke, an older boy from a nearby farm with whom I had sometimes walked to school, had been listening at the door, like a character out of a cheap spy novel. He had heard the whole thing and couldn't wait to spread the word. The "devil" had made contact! Scandal on the 11th Concession!

I can only imagine what happened to that poor teacher who stuck her neck out. My grandfather and a few others of similar sentiment were on the school board. There would be no sympathy. She stuck it out the rest of the school year, obviously under a dark cloud, but was not rehired. If she is still alive and reads this, thank you. You have no idea the joy you brought to a little boy.

The matter was never mentioned around me again, either by the teacher, my grandfather or Aunt Lila. Even John Hawke kept his mouth shut, perhaps a little embarrassed at being a snitch.

My father was partially correct: I did start to get some presents from him, but no letters got through. The presents at first were colourfully illustrated Bible stories in comic-book form. They were filled with battle scenes and heroes, and I devoured them. Thank goodness Lila never read anything but the Bible and thus was not aware of the graphic depictions in those comic books, especially those of the scantily clad, wanton Delilah tricking poor old Samson into cutting his hair.

My father had surmised that Lila would be more likely to accept Bible stories, even in comic-book form, than letters from him, but the most critical persuasion, I suspect, came from the American Red Cross which had arranged for the letter to reach my teacher. They threatened to have the monthly support cheques from the US Army stopped if the Wainmans didn't allow my father to communicate with me. That obviously caught their attention! The Canadian Red Cross, by the way, refused to help my father in his efforts to reach Phyllis and me. He never forgot or forgave them.

· · ·

Mom and Dad, Lowell's grandparents, celebrate their 50th wedding anniversary.

1956, Lowell has started his broadcast career and tells his grandfather he's going to take over from Gordon Sinclair!

Dad's 90th birthday. Left side of the table: Willard, Lowell, Dad and Genevieve; right side: Ken, Orlo, Nilah and her husband, Lloyd.

Dad and some of his great-grandchildren on his 90th birthday.

My sister Phyllis keeps smiling, no matter what fate throws in her path. She has not had an easy life, raising two sons and a daughter almost entirely alone on a meagre salary, but you would be hard-pressed to find anyone who enjoys life more. She now lives in Mission, BC, where she dotes on four grandchildren and volunteers for the Canadian Cancer Society.

Part II

The Guinea Pig

By the time my grandchildren have reached my age, I hope they have learned that life takes many strange twists and turns. I say hope because any life that does not travel some strange and often bumpy roads is a life not lived to the fullest. Even the smoothest of highways has curves for no other reason than to prevent boredom and keep the driver from falling asleep!

The *Ottawa Citizen* once asked me what I would like written on my tombstone. I surprised myself because, without even thinking, I replied instantly: "He took part!" It was intended as a fun article and most of it was, but I was very serious about my chosen epitaph. I confess to making some really stupid mistakes over the years, but choosing a smooth sleep-inducing highway for a life is not one of them.

Some of these long and winding roads are potholed with detours of varying lengths and degrees of difficulty. It was on one of these detours of life that I found myself, of all places, at the very Toronto radio station whose weak signal up there in Stumptown, Grandpa Green's ear would be glued each night, shushing us into silence to hear the grim war news. He, of course, had long since gone to meet his beloved Mom in a better life.

When I arrived at CFRB, there was no trace of Jim Hunter, the newscaster Henry Green trusted second only to God. Try as I might, I could find no one who knew anything about Hunter's musical signature—ta dum dum ta dum dum ta dum de dum de dum. When I went into the musical archives to search for it, the 18-year-old girl in charge gave me a weird look.

Gone, too, was any evidence of CFRB's most famous alumnus Lorne Greene (yes, Pa Cartwright on those reruns of "Bonanza"), but lo and behold, sitting at the desk in the little office assigned to me was the typewriter once used by the late Gordon Sinclair. I knew this, because there scratched into the surface, presumably by Gordon himself, were the words, "Gordon Sinclair." The typewriter was covered with dust. Certain it would inspire me, I dusted it off and used it reverentially every day.

Mr. Sinclair was long gone before any of my grandchildren were born, but for many years he was one of the most famous of all Canadians. His stories about travels through India and Europe enthralled me as a boy. As a broadcaster he was my idol. One of my proudest moments was the time I appeared on the television show "Front Page Challenge" with Gordon Sinclair, Betty Kennedy and Pierre Berton, three of Canada's most famous authors and broadcasters.

I was one of the mystery guests on the show. The panelists had three minutes to correctly identify the story the guest represented. My story was a real toughie. CFRA, the Ottawa radio station where I've spent most of my life, sent me to Vandenburgh Airforce Base in California to broadcast the launch into space of Canada's first satellite, Alouette 1.

Today, of course, launches of space satellites are almost a daily occurrence. In September of 1962, however, this was very exciting stuff indeed. In fact, Canada was the first nation after the USSR

September, 1962—History is about to be made. Alouette 1 sits atop that rocket, poised to blast off from Vandenberg Air Force Base in California. Canada was the third nation in the world to have a satellite circling the globe and Lowell was there to broadcast the event live. The recording is now in the National Archives. The man on the left is unknown, but to the right is the late Dr. John Chapman, the project manager and the man acknowledged as the father of Canada's satellite program.

and the US to build and have a satellite whirling around the planet. My live broadcast from the desert of Southern California is the only one ever made and now rests in the National Archives. But the reason they wanted me on "Front Page Challenge" was because of a crazy story I uncovered and exposed while covering the launch.

While poking around the nightlife of the town nearest to the air base, Santa Maria (yes, now home to Michael Jackson), I picked up some strange rumours about a little train that chugged right through the centre of the launch site. According to what I was hearing, this train, loaded down with fruit from nearby farms, had no set schedule and often disrupted launch programs. Vibrations from the train could jar delicate technical calibrations, plus there was always the fear that spies could stow aboard one of the freight cars and gain access to highly restricted areas.

Regardless of whether a launch was in the final countdown,

if the train—which I dubbed the "Citrus Special"—huffed and puffed onto the base, everything ground to a maddening, tear-your-hair-out halt. This often resulted in a total scrub of the launch, which cost hundreds of thousands of dollars and pretty well doubled the blood pressure of the entire launch crew.

I did some research, found the story to be true and reported it back to CFRA news director Campbell McDonald. Campbell thought I was crazy at first, but thankfully the station carried the story. While ignored by the staid *Ottawa Citizen*, it was printed in the *Ottawa Journal*.

Any skepticism was quickly extinguished the next night when, with only a few minutes to go before the launch of Alouette 1, sure enough onto the base rattled the Citrus Special, accompanied by the usual helicopters, whose high powered searchlights turned midnight in the California desert into high noon. The choppers and their lights followed the train until it was well off the site. By that time, the launch window had been lost and that day's planned launch of Alouette 1 had to be scrubbed.

The launch went off without a hitch the next night, but the wire services picked up my story. Before you knew it, it launched something else: a pitched battle on the floor of the US Senate. The idea that a little fruit train was costing the US military millions of dollars was scandalous to senators whose constituents weren't fruit farmers in southern California! The rail line was finally moved, and launches at Vandenburgh Air Force Base are no longer impacted by the Citrus Special.

The "Front Page Challenge" panelists didn't crack the story, but it was one of the great thrills of my life to meet three of the greatest broadcasters this country ever produced: Pierre Berton, Betty Kennedy and Gordon Sinclair.

Here I was broadcasting not only on the same radio station

Lowell, about to stump the "Front Page Challenge" panel, with host Fred Davis.

where those three worked, but the station that had played such an important role in our lives in that tiny kitchen in Stumptown. I was probably broadcasting from the same studio in which Jim Hunter sat. For all I knew, I was sitting in the same chair occupied by all of them—Jim Hunter, Lorne Greene, Betty Kennedy and Gordon Sinclair. And there in front of my flying fingers: the type-writer with which Gordon Sinclair wrote his daily scripts.

If only Henry and Mabel Green could see me now, I thought. How very proud they would be!

Toronto, as everyone knows, is pretty much the centre of the universe. Certainly the centre of Canada, as any Torontonian will quickly tell you. Everything isn't up-to-date in Toronto; it's ahead of the date! Thus I was surprised one day, not long after starting at CFRB, to spot an honest-to-goodness barbershop. Right there on Yonge Street, for heaven sakes, only a couple blocks south of our station on St. Clair. Not a salon, not a stylist, a barbershop! Combs bathing in blue liquid, electric clippers—hand-operated clippers! I swear there was even a razor strop hanging from one of the bulky chrome-encrusted barber chairs. Wooden chairs, obviously from the eighteenth century or maybe even prior, lined the walls; that morning's newspapers were strewn about. It brought back a flood of happy memories. I had to go in.

"Not too short," I instruct. "My wife will kill me if it's too short. Says my head is too big for short hair." Both barbers chuckle. "Haven't seen you around. You new here?" I can't resist. "Ya, I only started with CFRB a couple weeks ago." Three or four heads jerk up from newspapers. My barber stops cold in mid-scissor-snip. The other barber abandons his client's head and approaches. "You work for CFRB! What do you do?" "Talk shows, open-line shows." All activity stops. Both barbers now hover over me. The questions pound in.

An honest-to-goodness celebrity in their barber shop! Wait 'til the wife hears about this! The more they talk, the faster click the scissors about my head.

I get caught up in the whole thing. At last someone in Toronto seems to think I am a big deal! No one from CFRB had ever come into their shop before, they told me. What prompted me? So I tell them the story.

The year is 1945. The war is over. My father, discharged from the army, returns to Arthur where he rents the little house Bill Green had built. The house whose peak his grandmother Mary Ann had climbed to escape a wrathful mother. The house his father had been born in. He has a crazy idea that living in that house will provide him with sufficient inspiration to make a living writing.

By this time he has remarried and has two children with his new wife. Since no further military cheques are arriving, my mother allows Phyllis and I to visit him for the summer. *The Reader's Digest* and the *Toronto Weekly Star* are buying almost everything H. Gordon

Green writes, but it just isn't enough to feed all the mouths, so he takes a job teaching creative writing at the "rehab" school in Brockville.

This is a huge sprawling complex created by the government to help returning soldiers complete an education interrupted by the war. Every skill and profession under the sun is taught there—from welding to English literature, geography to barbering. Soldiers can pick up their education or training at whatever spot it was interrupted when they marched off to war. Students, teachers and professors all live together on campus in hastily assembled barracks, which are little more than cardboard boxes.

Because I have only just been reunited with my father after more than three years apart, it is decided and agreed upon by the school authorities that I can go and live with him on campus for a month.

I am shaking with excitement as that train pulls into Brockville and my father meets me with an old truck he has borrowed from someplace. He is living with two of his students and a pet spider, all crowded together in one small room. I take the top bunk bed, my father the lower. I forget who occupied the bottom rung of the other set of bunk beds, but the upper bunk is the property of Bud Lampman whose father is Archibald Lampman, Canada's poet laureate, something Bud doesn't seem all that impressed by, but my father certainly is.

Remember that movie about the boy king of China? That's the way I was treated everywhere. I was the only kid on campus. Everyone knew who I was, and I suspect knew a bit of my story. It was one very long way, believe me, from the 11th Concession, Orillia Township, and David and Lila Wainman!

The thing that intrigues me most about our cozy little hut is Bonaparte, Bud's pet spider. Since there are no locked doors on campus, Bonaparte has ballooned to truly enormous size, fed by a steady stream of the idle and curious who delight in watching him attack anything deposited on his web. From houseflies to one of last night's beans, Bonaparte does not discriminate! If it lands within his grasp it is grub. All eating and no work makes Bonaparte so portly he keeps breaking his web, strung between the wall and the heating radiator. Bud finally has to erect a small sign saying "Please do not feed the spider." No one pays any attention.

In the end, Bonaparte gives up mending his web, coming to the realization, just as with some humans, that if you don't feel like working for your dinner, someone else will provide it for you.

I learned a valuable lesson that summer, too: the law of supply and demand.

One of the advantages of the Brockville "rehab" school was free haircuts. That is, if you didn't mind something less than perfection. The large barber school on campus was in constant need of volunteers. The only way to learn to cut hair is to cut hair! They had no trouble finding sufficient numbers of students either so broke they couldn't afford experience, or so lacking in ego that a soup-bowl look didn't matter.

But remember, I am the only kid on campus, and a good chunk of a barber's business in the real world is with kids.

The first time they call me in and offer to cut my hair for free I don't mind, but after the third time in only a couple days, Bud Lampman pulls me aside to give me a bit of free advice. "How much money do you have?" he asks. I turn my pockets inside out. "See, you don't have any money do you? Every time you want an ice cream or pop, you've got to hit up your Dad or me. Look, the next time those guys in the barber shop call you in and want to practise cutting your hair, charge them a dime."

I am flabbergasted. "Charge them to cut my hair?"

Bud is persuasive. "Look, you don't need another haircut do

you? You've already had, what three?" I nod. "So, get smart. Your time is worth money, charge them a dime."

So it was that during that glorious summer just north of Brockville, I got to spend a whole month with my father, got my hair cut several dozen times and made almost three dollars. It doesn't get any better than that!

It certainly didn't get any better than that in that Toronto barber shop. I either put my barber to sleep or so enthralled him with my story that we both lost track of what was happening. I got clipped right down to the scalp.

My wife wouldn't talk to me for a week!

. . .

Viola

His name is Heber Gregg, known to all as Heberman. He's playing crazy eights with a five-year-old neighbour. Heberman is holding his cards in the inner crook of what is left of his right arm. With a grand flourish he yanks a card out with a battered left hand and slaps it down on a rickety old table with glee. "Gotcha!"

The little boy grabs a handful of cards and throws them high into the air as he leaps the three steps from the tiny porch into the dusty street. From a safe distance he taunts: "I got you, Heberman! I got you!" Heberman feigns a lunge towards the street. The little boy dances a few feet further away, then stops as the screen door slams. A very pretty, slim, blond girl in blue shorts and white blouse steps onto the porch, arms akimbo, fists on hips. "Daniel," she yells, "your mother just called. You were supposed to be home hours ago. Now git."

It's summer in Willow Village. I'm 12. She's 12. Right then and there, I fall in love!

By 1948, Willow Village is a sleepy little burg, just a few miles down the road from Ypsilanti, Michigan. It's home to a couple of thousand people at most.

You would never know that only three years ago this town and its adjacent Willow Run factory was known around the world as the "Arsenal of Democracy." It was right here that 8,685 B-24 Liberator bombers were built. By 1944, a Liberator was rolling off the assembly line every 56 minutes. A huge dormitory with 1,300 beds was erected just to accommodate the airmen required to fly the bombers to their various squadrons

The plant covered 3.5 million square feet, the largest factory in the world. Charles Lindbergh called it the Grand Canyon of the mechanized world. More than 42,000 people, most of them women, worked in the Willow Run plant. More than 100,000 people lived in what was supposed to be a temporary barracks-like housing development that shot up almost overnight.

Henry Ford, who built the plant, wanted to call the raw new town Bomber City, but since they were having difficulty recruiting sufficient workers, it was decided that Willow Village sounded more attractive.

The first plane was completed at Willow Run on October 1, 1942. It was christened "The Spirit of Ypsilanti." Its $300,000 cost was paid for with a fundraising drive by the townspeople of Ypsilanti, who bought war bonds and stamps. Contributors were issued buttons bearing the bomber's "Winged V" insignia, designed by a 17-year-old student at Ypsilanti High School.

When the final Liberator bomber rolled down the assembly line in late 1945, it was christened "The Henry Ford," but he objected and insisted that the plane be named after the workers who had built it. Henry Ford's name was erased from the plane and the workers autographed the nose.

Only a few hundred homes remained when I arrived that summer of 1948. Row housing, long and narrow. Three apartments per unit. Built almost overnight for Willow Run workers of cheap plywood covered with some kind of tarpaper made to look like panelling. Occupied for the most part now by pensioners and students from the University of Michigan in nearby Ann Arbor.

I learn all of this and much more from our next-door neighbour Heberman Gregg the first afternoon I arrive. "Left the rest of this here, four thousand feet down a Pennsylvania coal mine," he says, raising the stump of his right arm. It had been severed at about mid-forearm. "Back in '43 they was pretty desperate for bodies of any sort up here. My coal minin' days was over, so when old Henry Ford offered a bunch of us jobs in the frozen north, why we all jumped like bullfrogs. Mr. Ford I guess wasn't countin' arms so they brought our little family up here by bus and gave us this here nice little home." He chuckles. "Turns out I was the fastest one-armed riveter in all of Willow Run! Course I wasn't going to let the ladies beat me, was I now?"

Considering the constant distraction, it's a wonder I can recall anything of what he said. "Mary, what are you looking out for?" asks Heberman as his daughter, the one I had already decided to fall in love with that morning, peers out the screen door for about the fiftieth time since I'd been invited over for a Coke and a chat. "Just checking to see who's on the road," she says. Heberman gives me an eye twinkle. "I suspect it ain't the road you're checkin'." "Oh, Dad!" was all I hear and she disappears.

It was a wonderful summer romance. The first for both of us. Holding hands; the first awkward kiss; afternoons at the movies. The Greggs lived in the unit next to ours, separated only by walls so thin that Mary and I could talk to each other through them, and often did so half the night.

Her father was receiving a small disability pension, her mother Eva taught from time to time. They had very little money. Mary had lived all of her life in what we today would call poverty, but by no means did she consider herself poor or disadvantaged in anyway. Nobody in Willow Village had any money, which is why we were all there.

It was the lowest of low-cost housing. I think the rent was about $12 a month—about all I suspect we could handle. My father had given up on trying to make a living in Arthur and returned to the University of Michigan to obtain his Master's degree in English literature and write his first novel. The only income he had was from working the night shift at a nearby auto plant.

There were six of us crammed into that tiny apartment. My father and my stepmother Lillian (Lil), and my half-siblings Sidney and Marielle, and for the summer, Phyllis and I.

Mary had an older sister, Viola, who lived in Detroit. Viola had recently separated from her husband and invited Mary and me to visit her for a couple of days. It was there that I was confronted head-on for the first time with the issue of race. Growing up in southwestern Ontario, I doubt whether I had seen more than a half-dozen black people, or Negroes as we called them then. Race was not an issue back in Ontario, but it certainly was in Detroit, which in 1948 was one of the most racially segregated cities in the northern United States

Despite having spent a good deal of her childhood in Ku Klux Klan country in Georgia, Viola is deeply sympathetic to the plight of black people. The fact that blacks are denied the right to vote in some southern states, she finds especially galling.

When I express surprise at the discrimination I have seen on the streets of Detroit, both she and her best friend Sarah Evans spend the better part of an evening enlightening me on the facts of life for blacks in the United States of America.

Sarah is an African-American woman who cares for Viola's two children, Penny and Evangeline Mary, while their mother works at the Ford plant. Some of the things they tell me—the poverty, the separate drinking fountains, the separate movie theatre sections, the denial of basic human rights, including the right to vote in some states—astonish and anger me.

From the newspaper clippings they show me of cross burnings, lynchings and mutilations of black men, it is clear that for blacks in the deep south, the Ku Klux Klan is a fearsome terrorist organization.

I am certain that in that little Detroit apartment a spark of social conscience was ignited that made a career of battling the establishment inevitable for me.

And as for Viola? There was no way any of us could possibly have known the terrible tragedy that lay ahead for her.

It is Lil who gives me the news. She is sobbing on the phone. "Your Dad's in Newfoundland, can you take me to the funeral?" I have no idea what she is talking about. "Lil, Lil, what's the matter? Who's funeral?" "Viola's," she says. There is a pause, "You don't know?" "Lil, I have no idea what's happening, Viola who?"

"Viola Luizzo, you remember, Mary Gregg's sister." Her voice takes on a bitter, angry edge. "The damn Klan shot her. Murdered her in cold blood. Your Dad and I have been invited to the funeral."

Lil had become close friends with Viola. Only a few months prior to her death Viola, facing a personal crisis, came to my father's farm at Ormstown, Quebec, to spend some time with Lil. It was a spur-of-the-moment decision, and unfortunately, Lil was in New Brunswick visiting her parents when Viola arrived.

My half-sister Marielle says that Viola had lost a child and was disconsolate. Marielle stayed with her until Lil arrived back home. In gratitude, Viola gave Marielle her diamond engagement ring from her first marriage, something Marielle cherishes to this day.

There is no official record of Viola losing a child. Whether it was a miscarriage or a stillbirth seems unclear. All that Marielle remembers is that Viola was very upset and very grateful for the solace that both she and Lil provided.

The murder of Viola Luizzo, a civil rights volunteer on a lonely road near Selma, Alabama, was front-page news around the world. As chief news editor of radio station CFRA in Ottawa, I wrote and broadcast the story and subsequent developments dozens of times. But until the phone call from Lil, I had no idea that the Viola Luizzo who had become a martyr to the civil rights movement was the same Mary Gregg's sister Viola who had challenged my conscience 17 years earlier.

No story better illustrates the struggle for equal rights that dominated most of the '60s than that of Viola Luizzo. The events, which culminated in the cowardly murder of Viola, began in late February 1965 when police, during a voter rights demonstration in Selma, Alabama, killed Jimmy Lee Jackson, a young African-American. In anger, Dr. Martin Luther King Jr., the great civil rights leader of the 1960s and '70s, organized a march to be held on March 7 in Selma.

In his book, *Selma 1965*, Charles E. Fager describes the march as follows:

> *After Dr. King announced the planned march down route 80 from Selma to Montgomery, the capital of Alabama, Governor George Wallace banned the march and called out state troopers to block their path, despite assurances from*

march leaders that the demonstration would be peaceful.

As the 600 marchers moved out from Brown Chapel African Church and started across the Pettus Bridge, they could see the line of troopers spread shoulder to shoulder blocking the highway.

At the command "troopers advance" they charged into the marchers swinging billy clubs. The younger marchers escaped. The elderly were knocked to the pavement, wooden clubs thudding into their flesh. When other marchers came to their aid, they were sprayed with clouds of tear gas. A sheriff's posse on horseback joined the fray using bullwhips, ropes and lengths of rubber tubing covered with barbed wire while pursuing the marchers through downtown.

Network television captured the assault on Highway 80 for a shocked American public, clearly showing the peaceful marchers, the failing police clubs, the stampeding horses, the jeering onlookers and the stricken fleeing blacks.

In Atlanta, an infuriated Dr. King sent out telegrams to every prominent clergyman sympathetic to the black cause, reading in part, "In the vicious maltreatment of defenseless citizens of Selma, where old women and young children were gassed and clubbed at random, we have witnessed an eruption of the disease of racism which seeks to destroy all America. No American is without responsibility. The people of Selma will struggle on for the soul of the nation but it is fitting that all Americans help to bear the burden. I call therefore on clergy of all faiths to join me in Selma.

Religious groups from around the country sent representatives, "nuns in flowing habits, rabbinical students with their yarmulkes, white collared clergy from every denomination," according to one Detroit News *story.*

Ordinary people horrified by the attacks went to Selma to add their voices to the cry for justice. One who answered the call was a Detroit housewife, Viola Luizzo, 39, wife of a Teamster Union employee and mother of five.

King and the Southern Christian Leadership Conference had won a court order allowing the march from Selma to Montgomery and directing the state to protect the marchers. However, the order limited the march to 300 people on a section of Highway 80 that was only two lanes wide. Governor Wallace told the White House the state couldn't afford to pay the cost of mobilizing the National Guard for the march, giving President Johnson the opportunity he was looking for. He federalized 1,900 of Alabama's National Guard, authorized the use of 2,000 regular army troops as well as 200 FBI agents and U.S. Marshals to protect the marchers.

The Selma-Montgomery march started on March 21, the marchers camping at night wherever they could. Finally they arrived in Montgomery on March 24.

As they neared Montgomery, the road widened, ending the 300-person limitation, and all through the afternoon cars and buses stopped along the line and discharged new marchers. There were thousands of them, exuberant and noisy, carrying banners and placards. When they arrived at the final campsite the march was like a tide coming in, inevitable and relentless, inundating everything.

Viola Luizzo had come to Selma a week previous after watching on television the vicious attack on the defenseless marchers on the Pettus Bridge. Her best friend, African-American Sara Evans, told the *Detroit News* later Viola decided the time had come to stop talking about helping and actually do something. Her husband didn't want her to go, warning her it could be dangerous, but Viola could not be deterred. It took her three days to drive from Detroit to Selma where she was immediately put to work ferrying marchers and other supporters back and forth from Selma to the airport in Montgomery.

Viola had driven to Montgomery the final night of the march to join the triumphant entry into the state capital. She helped in the first-aid station with the worn-out marchers or those who had fainted from the heat and exertion. She and Father Tim Deasy climbed a tower to view the marchers. The line stretched out, filling the street completely with no end in sight heading toward the Capitol Building. She told Deasy she had a premonition: "Something is going to happen today, I feel it, somebody is going to get killed…" She repeated her premonition to another priest and a group of nuns.

All the important civil rights fighters were in the march: Dr. King, his wife Coretta Scott King, Roy Wilkins of the National Association for the Advancement of Colored People (NAACP), Whitney Young of the Urban League, Ralph Bunche, the Nobel Peace Prize winner, and Rosa Parks who started the civil rights movement when she refused to move to the back of a bus.

Dr. King delivered one of his most famous speeches: "How long will it take? …Not long, because mine eyes have seen the glory of the coming of the Lord." King tried to deliver a petition calling for full voting rights to Governor Wallace, but troopers kept him out of the Capitol Building.

After the march ended, thousands had to get out of the city before nightfall. There was no place for them to stay and many feared for their safety. Viola Luizzo retrieved her car, loaded it up with several passengers and headed back to Selma.

There was danger on the road. Her Michigan licence plates were a target and now the army troops that had protected the marchers were gone. At one point a carload of whites came up behind her car and bumped it. She commented to Leroy Moton, a black teenager who had been helping her to drive, that she thought these local white folks were crazy.

As soon as their passengers were dropped off at Brown Chapel in Selma, Viola and Leroy headed back to Montgomery to pick up another load of passengers. On the way out of town, they stopped at a traffic light and another car pulled up alongside. In it were four Ku Klux Klansmen from Bessemer, a steel town near Birmingham. One passenger in the car was FBI informant Gary Rowe who was sitting in the back seat. Collie Leroy Wilkins looked out his window and saw Mrs. Luizzo and her black companion stopped beside them. "Look there, baby brother," Wilkins said to Rowe, "I'll be damned. Look there."

Eugene Thomas, who was driving the Klan car, said, "Let's get them." When the light changed they began chasing the Michigan car, careening through the darkened swamps of Lowndes County at almost 100 miles per hour. Rowe would later say on the witness stand that he repeatedly tried to persuade the other two to give up the chase but that Thomas insisted, "We're not going to give up, we're going to take that car."

As the Klansmen closed in on their prey, Thomas pulled out a pistol, handed it to Wilkins and told the others to draw their own weapons. Rowe says he tried once more to get them to stop, but Thomas said, "I done told you, baby brother, you're in the big time now." A moment later they pulled alongside their quarry. Wilkins put his arm out through the window. Mrs. Luizzo turned and looked straight at him and he fired twice through the glass of her window. The fourth Klansman, William Eaton, emptied his pistol at the car. Rowe claimed he only pretended to fire his weapon. Then their car sped away.

Viola Luizzo fell against the wheel, dead instantly from two bullets to the head. Leroy Moton was splattered with blood but managed to grab the steering wheel and hit the brakes. The car veered to the right, crashed through a ditch and came to rest against an embankment.

Moton turned off the lights and ignition and tried to rouse Mrs. Luizzo. As he realized she was dead, he saw the other car come back and pull up beside them. He played dead as the Klansmen shined a light into the car, then drove away. Moton left the car and began running down the highway towards Montgomery until he spotted a truck he recognized as belonging to a fellow marcher. He climbed in, told what had happened to them, and then passed out cold.

Within 24 hours, President Johnson was on television, personally announcing the arrest of the four assailants and vowing to eliminate the KKK.

Viola's body was returned to Detroit on March 27. A *Detroit News* reporter visited the home where her husband Anthony and children Penny, 18, Thomas, 13, Anthony Jr., 10, and Sally, 6, were trying to cope. Another daughter, Mrs. Evangeline Mary Johnson, was on her way from Georgia. Viola's sister Mary, yes, the same Mary I had fallen in love with 17 years before, was doing her best to care for the youngest children.

Mary and I had lost track of each other over the years, but Viola stayed in touch with my father and Lil, both of whom were invited to attend her wedding in 1951 when she married Anthony Luizzo, a union organizer for the Teamsters. The invitation for the Greens to attend Viola's funeral was at the request of Anthony who valued their friendship greatly.

As far as I know, Lil was the only Canadian at the funeral. My father was in Newfoundland researching a book and couldn't get plane reservations. I was unable to drive Lil from their farm at

Ormstown, Quebec, to Detroit. Undeterred, she recruited a young neighbour's son to help her drive and they set out in that old Buick Roadmaster headed west. The Buick (yes, the same one we used to rescue Frank Selke's chickens) finally gave up the ghost in Brantford.

Here's something you may find hard to believe but is absolutely true. Lil left home in such a hurry that she had almost no money with her, no credit cards and no cheques. The Buick refused to move an inch out of Brantford; it was getting late in the day, the funeral was the next morning in Detroit and she was determined to be there. She walked into a store, asked to use the phone, got the number for a local GM car dealer, got the sales manager on the phone and, incredibly, had a new car delivered within half an hour without handing over a cent!

At the time, my father had a syndicated radio program called the "Old Cynic." It was carried on a number of Canadian radio stations, including CKPC Brantford. When the car dealership sales manager learned that he was talking with the Old Cynic's wife, he gave her a brand new Chevy with the promise that she would mail him a cheque when she got home! I swear on a stack of Bibles that story is true.

My father had to scramble to round up the $4,000-plus required to pay for the car when he got home. Not only did the dealership get the sale of the car, they got coast-to-coast advertising from my father who for once had to drop the Old Cynic's pose and admit there were still some pretty fine people in the world!

Lil and the neighbour's boy drove well into the night before finally arriving in Detroit. They had no idea where they were in that dark and dangerous city. They found themselves in some kind of warehouse area where they spotted a pay phone and called my Uncle Cecil who lived in nearby St. Clair Shores.

Cecil was very worried. "Where are you?" he asked. Lil wasn't sure but was able to tell him the names of the two nearest inter-secting streets. There was a sharp intake of breath from Cecil. "Get into that car right now," he instructed. "Lock all your doors, turn off the lights and don't make a sound. I'll be there as soon as I can." Clearly, they had arrived in one of Detroit's more unsavoury districts.

Cecil performed the rescue successfully, and the next day Lil was one of more than 750 people, including Dr. Martin Luther King, who attended a high Requiem mass for Viola at the Immaculate Heart of Mary Roman Catholic Church. The day previous, March 29, the NAACP sponsored a memorial service for Viola at the People's Community Church. More than 1,500 attended, including Rosa Parks and other leading civil rights workers of the day. Both services were televised nationwide.

Because one of those in the Klan car was Gary Rowe, a FBI informant, the role of the FBI was drawn into question. In an effort to extradite his organization from the controversy, Director J. Edgar Hoover, one of the most evil men in American history, began a slander campaign against Viola, claiming among other things that she had only gone to Alabama to sleep with civil rights workers and had abandoned her children.

Hoover's efforts are one of the most disgraceful chapters in the entire civil rights movement and caused Viola's family, especially her husband and children, great pain. In the end, Hoover was the one discredited, and Viola Luizzo is today recognized as one of the great martyrs of the civil rights movement.

As Kay Houston wrote in the *Detroit News*, "Viola Luizzo was a Detroit housewife who moved a nation towards racial justice."

As brief as our acquaintance was, I can honestly say I am proud to have known her.

• • •

Pork Chops and Confederation

Of all the things in the world likely to be involved in political intrigue, you would think pork chops would be mighty low on the list. Not so. Not so at all. In fact, my father tried to delay the final confederation of Canada and barely escaped going to jail over pork chops. Well not actually just pork chops—but bacon and ham and everything else that goes into the making of a pig.

That lovely tower of pork chops that I risked both the wrath of God and Grandfather to plunder came from our little Stumptown farm on the edge of Arthur. "Homegrown to beat the band," as he would say. "We breed them, we feed them and then they feed us." Which was pretty well the way it was right across Canada when I was growing up.

We were mostly a nation of small family farms then. Wonderfully self-sufficient. We grew and raised enough of just about everything to feed our own family, and if we had a bit left-over we hauled it off to the local "Saturday Market" where the less fortunate (or so we believed) city dwellers would stock up for the week.

It was a time, of course, before the government had invented all the deadly diseases that would befall anyone eating uninspected or unlicensed meat or produce. So everything from live chickens, rabbits and pigeons to whole sides of beef and pork were sold completely unadorned with stamps, tags or certificates of approval. One thing about war is that it so wonderfully occupies government minds that they pretty well leave the folks at home alone to look out for themselves. It was a time, as well, when people cared too much about each other to even think of selling anything that might make anyone sick, so it worked out just fine and no one seemed to be bothered too much by the flies!

With the war over, however, governments began to look around for something to feed their ever-increasing appetite for more money, more employees and more control over our lives, and perhaps just as importantly, to justify their very existence. Before you could say Jack Robinson, all sorts of new departments and agencies sprang up, all of which they claimed would help us. If someone asked what you were doing, you could always get a good laugh by replying, "I'm from the government and I'm here to help!"

One of these departments, heaven only knows which one, came up with the theory that the bacon Canadians were eating was too fatty. If you were a farmer you could easily burn off a pound of bacon grease just tossing a set of harness over the backs of a team of grumpy horses every morning. But as more and more Canadians abandoned barns for bright city lights, the fat was beginning to appear in some unwanted places, including ladies' thighs and men's tummies. The government really didn't care about that, but when Canadians started buying imported lean bacon and hams from Denmark, one of the new government departments informed another government department that it was hurting the Canadian hog industry. Neither department really cared about any of that either; in fact, they were delighted they actually had something to report. Nor was there great concern when another government department announced that since Canadian hog producers weren't making as much money, less tax could be collected. Only when another government department discovered that less tax collected placed civil service wage increases at risk did the alarm bells go off.

Now any normal person would look at the situation and say, look, Canadian consumers are buying Danish bacon and ham because it's leaner. So let's get some of those leaner Danish hogs over here so we can create a level playing field for Canadian farmers.

Governments, of course, are not normal. Instead of simply going to Denmark and buying up a bunch of these leaner pigs, which by the way were and still are called Landrace hogs, our government launched yet another department whose job it was to create our own Canadian longer, leaner pig to compete with the Danes. And just to ensure that the government's reputation for screwing everything up perfectly was not jeopardized, they actually passed a law making it illegal to import a single Danish Landrace hog into Canada. In 1947, importing one Landrace hog into the country would get you a longer jail term than holding up the local bank!

This "magical" all-Canadian pig, announced the federal government, would be created at the Agricultural Experimental Station in Lacombe, Alberta. In another burst of inventive genius, they revealed that this marvellous new beast, which just like the Landrace would have an extra set of ribs to give us more and leaner bacon, would be called, you guessed it, the Lacombe. "And by the way, yes it is true," admitted the government, "among the breeds used to create this new wonderhog were several Landrace hogs, imported by the Canadian government!" When someone pointed out the fact that Landrace hogs had just been declared illegal by the same government that now claimed ownership of several, the Landrace mysteriously disappeared from Lacombe and presumably from the face of the earth!

My father fought the odds, stupidity and convention all his life, and having pioneered the importation of Galloway cattle into Canada, it was only natural that he would take up the cause of Landrace hogs. With the inflamed blood of Vikings flowing through his veins, spurred on by his new Danish wife, he convinced himself this had become personal and, by God, he wasn't going to take it! He came stomping up dusty Côte St. Francois one bleak day in November, slapped the Danish National

Gordon Green on his farm near Ste-Thérèse greets one of the smuggled immigrants (the Landrace sow) that revolutionized the hog industry in Canada. You can also tell Landrace by their long lean sides (better for bacon) and their floppy ears.

Belted Galloway cattle on our farm at Ashton. Wonderful to look at, but the fence to hold them has yet to be invented!

Anthem onto his old crank-up record player, turned the volume up full blast, opened the windows wide so everyone could hear and then, armed with a hammer, marched out the back door, nailed a huge Danish flag to his little barn and declared all-out war on the Canadian Government.

The government should have given up right then and there and begged Denmark for boatloads of Landrace hogs. But don't let anyone fool you, governments were no smarter in those days than they are today. So naturally they continued merrily along spending millions of tax dollars trying to invent a pig that was already rooting up the hog hollows of Denmark.

My father, as one of the editors of the *Family Herald*, the bible of Canadian agriculture, was a bit of a hero in the farming community. It was true not only in this country but in parts of Europe as well, that some of his stories, books and articles had been published in several different languages. In short, he had a lot of contacts, some of whom had some political pull, and better yet, some of whom had a bit of larceny in their souls. Too much larceny as it turned out in one case.

Somehow my father managed to get several Landrace hogs smuggled out of Denmark and into Britain. He wasn't quite sure how he was going to get them from Britain to Canada, but figured customs officials would be far less suspicious of swine arriving from Manchester then they would those coming in from Copenhagen. They got to Britain, all right, then very mysteriously disappeared. My father, as you can imagine, was mad as hell. The adventure had cost him several thousand dollars and he was pretty sure he knew who the hognapper was. Problem was he could hardly go to the authorities. What would he say? Someone has stolen my smuggled pigs! You get the point. Kiss those babies goodbye and start all over again.

And then a brainwave. On July 22, 1948, in a second referendum held that year, slightly more than 52 percent of Newfoundlanders voted to cease being a de facto colony of Great Britain and join Canada. The official ceremony was to take place on March 31, 1949, with Joey Smallwood to be sworn in as the new province's first premier on April 1.

On March 14, my father phoned Joey Smallwood to ask a small favour. "I've got two bred Landrace sows ready to be shipped from Denmark to St. John's, Newfoundland," he explained to the puzzled Joey. "They should arrive there about the first week in April. If you can delay signing that final agreement to join Canada for a couple of weeks, Newfoundland will still be a British colony when they arrive. Then, after you sign the agreement, they'll be in Canada legally." It was a stroke of pure genius. Except, of course, for the timing.

History records that Joey Smallwood turned my father down flatly. Newfoundland joined Confederation as scheduled on March 31, 1949. Joey Smallwood became its first premier on April 1. 'Til the day he died, my father was flabbergasted at Joey's refusal. "He'd been a pig farmer himself," lamented my father. "Surely he of all people should have understood what was at stake. Hell, what difference would it have made to delay Confederation a week or two?"

Years later while interviewing Joey Smallwood, I related the story and asked Joey if he recalled the phone call. Joey stared at me for several moments, unblinking through those owl glasses of his. "That was your father?!" I nodded. He shook his head slightly. "I thought the man was mad!"

History also records that, in the end, my father won the war. One fine morning in 1953, a small herd of Landrace hogs ambled out of a farmyard in Maine. They wandered along, as pigs are wont to do when undisturbed, until they were met a few hundred yards up the road by a farmer who calmly pointed their snouts in the direction of his farmyard, in New Brunswick. The pigs—unconcerned with borders or nationality—thought the corn on the Canadian side of the road was just as tasty as that in the US. In fact, the Yankees hadn't fed them a lot of corn, whereas it was piled high in Canada.

My father, when confronted by the police and other assorted authorities in the months to come, always insisted the pigs had just decided on their own to come to Canada, and that once here he was as entitled to them as anyone. I was there on Côte St. Francois as excited as anyone when that big truck bearing New Brunswick licence plates pulled into our driveway and out piled the longest, leanest, most floppy-eared pigs anyone had ever seen. My father had rehearsed a few words of Danish to greet them and they really seemed to appreciate it.

We tried to keep it a secret, but within days farmers begging for the pick of the first litter besieged our little farm north of Montreal. Some offered outrageous amounts of money for one—or the lot—of them. My father could have made a small fortune right then and there, but he was having too much fun. The government inspectors and other assorted officialdom arrived, some bearing writs and threats and dire warnings. But nothing came of it; it was all wind and dust.

More Landrace made that little stroll down a country lane between Maine and New Brunswick. The ban on importation was finally lifted, and today there is hardly a pig in all of Canada, North America for that matter, that isn't either a Landrace or has Landrace blood in it.

They finally did create a Lacombe hog, but it came nowhere near to matching the Landrace for making fine, lean ham and bacon, and I suspect the breed has long since died out. When John

Candy made the movie *Canadian Bacon*, that was Landrace bacon they were referring to, the famous bacon now sold around the world—even to Denmark! The bacon has made millions for the hog industry in this country and, indirectly of course, the government. My father's picture should be on every package.

• • •

To give you an idea of how valuable those first few Landrace hogs were, let me tell you a story of how I once made a grown man cry.

The year is 1956, I have just graduated from Macdonald Agricultural School in Ste. Anne de Bellevue on the West Island of Montreal. I'm at loose ends for a few days, so when a friend of my father's asks if I could do a "little job" for him, I agree. The little job involves flying to Moncton, New Brunswick, where a very pregnant Landrace sow has just arrived from Denmark and is just now being cleared from quarantine. I'm to get it cleared through customs, out of quarantine, and insure that it arrives safely into the bosom of its owner, Larry Lalonde, proprietor of the Farmer's Co-op store in Brockville. "You've got to treat her with kid gloves," instructs Larry. "She's very pregnant and don't forget each one of her piglets is worth $300." Remember, in 1956, $300 is a lot of money.

I won't go into the sad details of my flight to Moncton. Suffice to say it was a tiny plane buffeted by every breeze, and I had foolishly involved myself in a giant graduation party the night before! The mere mention of the world Moncton today makes me shudder.

I do finally arrive and make my way to the quarantine station where the lady in waiting is waiting. Small problem: she's not pregnant anymore. She's just given birth to eight squirming little piglets whose desire for food is surpassed only by the aforementioned crows.

One of the problems with pigs is that they aren't too smart, especially around their babies. Sows also tend to be rather large and prone to sudden, without warning, lie-downs whenever and wherever the spirit moves them. Evolution has equipped the piglets with a sensory system able to detect the impending motherly descent, but if not provided with a space under which they can sprint to safety, the results can be very young sausage!

With the help of a couple of local "lads," we rigged up a crate that provided just such an escape hatch, and I went back to the hotel feeling pretty proud of myself. Survived a giant party, terrible flight and a birthing, all within 24 hours.

To this day I am not sure why I didn't phone Larry Lalonde back in Brockville to give him the joyous news. He was, after all, the proud owner now of not only a Landrace sow, but eight wonderful little piglets worth $300 each—a small fortune in those days. Instead, I fired off a telegram, dictating it very carefully to the telegraph operator: "Sow fine, gave birth, eight pigs alive."

It is a slightly demented Larry Lalonde who phones my hotel room at about three in the morning. He has obviously been drinking heavily and is fluctuating wildly between sobs and screams of rage. "Kill the son of a bitch," he sobs. "Kill the son of a bitch," he screams, growing more incoherent by the second. "Larry, Larry," I manage to say, "what are you talking about? What's the matter with you?" He is sobbing again. "What the hell kind of a pig would eat her own? Kill the son of a bitch. I don't want ever to see her again."

I am having trouble now understanding what he is saying. "Larry," I ask, "what do you mean ate her pigs? She's got eight pigs that are doing fine." Then it hits me! "Oh no," I groan, "that bloody telegram, what does it say?" There is a rustle at the other end of the line. "I've got it right here. It says, "'Sow fine, gave birth, ate pigs alive.'" Then there is a pause. "What do you mean there are eight pigs alive? You said she ate them."

"Larry, for goodness sakes man, she didn't eat the pigs, she's got eight pigs that are alive! They spelled eight—"a-t-e"—it's not ate, it's eight." I spell out the letters—e-i-g-h-t—eight pigs alive. "Larry, you've got nine pigs here—one mother and eight fine and dandy little pigs."

I have never heard a man sober up so fast. Before you know it, he has his wife on the phone and is making me repeat the eight and the ate again and again, laughing, yelling, then finally leaving me dangling on the phone as they do a little dance up the hall.

By the time I got his nine pigs to Brockville the next night, the entire town had heard the story or versions of it. For years I couldn't go near the place without people stopping me on the street and saying something like, "So Lowell, how do you spell eight?"

Portable Pete

It's the fall of 1954, 11 years since my little introductory scrap with Whitey Green in the schoolyard of the Lake St. George School near Orillia, and it's happening again! We've all just arrived at the Annex of the Men's Residence of Macdonald College in Ste-Anne-de-Bellevue, our home for the next two years. I don't even have my stuff unpacked and here's this funny little guy with a weird brush cut dancing around, urging me to fight some guy named Bob Boreham. Believe me, I want no part of this Mr. Boreham.

Bob Boreham is one big bruiser. Outweighs me at least by 20 pounds and has a fist the size of a scoop shovel. He's just come out of the mines of Asbestos, Quebec, as hard as a block of granite. And, just as with Whitey Green more than a decade ago, Bob wants no part of me either. But this crazy little guy is shouting and hopping around like a monkey in the corridor, insisting that Boreham and Green go at it. He starts calling me "Lushwell," a name I'm stuck with for the rest of my stay at Macdonald. Pointing to the sporty new yellow shoes I thought were pretty neat, he says, "Fruit boots."

To tell the truth, I want to lay out the little guy, but Bob Boreham and I decide that in order to shut him up and give the growing chorus of others gathering around a bit of a show, we'd go a round or two. So there in the hallway of our new home, with most of our new classmates cheering us on, we pound each other a few times. I take what feels like a side of beef to the ear; he takes a pretty good rap on the nose. We look at each other, start to laugh and it's over. You women, I know, when reading this, will just roll your eyes skyward and say with exasperation, "Men!"

Bob Boreham, nicknamed "Tex," in recognition of the Stetson hat he loved to wear, became a friend. The asbestos he inhaled as a young man caught up with him and he died only months after hosting a class reunion at his home in Elliot Lake in 2004.

The "crazy little guy" with the brush cut who egged us on that first day at Macdonald was Peter Haydon. Grandson of Senator Andrew Haydon and brother of Andy Haydon who for several years was chairman of the Regional Government in Ottawa and after whom Andrew Haydon Park in Ottawa is named.

We had a vague idea that "Pete" was well-connected somehow, and the fact that his mother had loaned him a brand new 1954 Ford was pretty impressive, but the manner in which he became semi-legendary at Macdonald had nothing to do with his ancestry.

Pete was one of those guys who seemed to be everywhere. Drop into Joe's, the local drinking parlour, and there would be Pete ordering up a Red Cap. In fact, he didn't have to order. One of his prize processions was a railway engineer's cap with the words Red Cap printed in bold letters under the brim. Flip up the brim and his order was in. If you stopped by for a game of billiards in the basement of the men's residence, there was Pete taking some poor guy to the cleaners. I never saw him lose. He knew all the latest dances and introduced us to rock 'n' roll. It was from Pete that I first heard of Elvis Presley. "No guy by the name of Elvis Presley is going anywhere," he said. Attend the Green and Gold Review, the annual Macdonald theatre production, and there is Peter Haydon sliding down a rope onto the stage to deliver a line. I turn out for basketball and there is Pete, all five feet four inches of him, making the team as our star point guard.

Almost any night, Pete and his fellow Ottawan and roommate Neil Sorley can be glimpsed (briefly) pounding full tilt down a corridor of the residence with screams of outrage in hot pursuit. Pete has declared war on what he called the wimp teachers-in-training who inhabited the floor just above us, and Neil has obviously signed up for the battle. God help any student teacher that left residence for a weekend or even a day. His bed and sometimes all of his furniture might be found, after a frantic search, dangling from the upper balcony of the gym. Even a few minutes in the coffee shop could be disastrous. One of their favourite tricks was to tangle a guy's bedding out the window with a sign pinned to it with the victim's name and the word "filthy" scrawled in black crayon.

Most of us were involved in various types of hijinks. I have to confess that I was involved one early morning in hoisting Gilbert Koury's mini-car up the stairs of the men's residence and into the main lobby where we decorated it with various plants. None of this seemed to impress Gilbert very much. I will never forget the look of shock, amazement and amusement on the face of the *Montreal Gazette* delivery truck driver. Five a.m. and four guys pushing a car up a flight of stairs isn't something you see everyday. No one, though, enjoyed tweaking the noses of authority (and student teachers) more than Peter Haydon did.

I felt somewhat honoured when he approached me one day with an invitation. "I'm starting a new club," he said. "I'm inviting a few friends to join. You're the first." As it turns out, I actually *was* the first one he invited, because I was the first one he saw after dreaming it up. Everyone else was given exactly the same line with the same sincerity, including the last guy he invited. "What's the club?" I asked. "The Taboo Club. Very exclusive." "What's that?" "Joe's tonight, seven o'clock," was all he would say.

Most of our class was there right on time and Pete was correct. The Taboo Club *was* very exclusive. Restricted to those who could gurgle down six quarts of beer (any brand) in an hour, and 1) stay alive, and 2) stay out from under the table.

Fortunately, although we called the big bottles of beer you could only buy in Quebec quarts, they didn't actually contain a full quart. If they did, it is highly doubtful I would be here this day to tell the tale. It was still, however, a lot of beer!

Pete, as you might expect, claimed he had already accomplished the six-quart feat, thus did not have to do a repeat. Besides which, he reminded us, we'd need him to keep track. Do the counting. He held up his hand to lower the volume of objections. "There's an initiation fee." We all groaned. "Anyone who signs up to join and craps out owes me a quart." He looked around. "Okay?"

He had his audience figured out. To object would have indicated we didn't think we could do it. "No problem," we said.

I don't recall much after that. But I was initiated into the Taboo Club that night, along with a few others. Pete held similar initiations almost every week. I do not believe he had to pay for a beer the entire year.

I know, I know, it's all pretty juvenile. But please remember we were only 18 or 19 and on our own for the first time. Attitudes towards drinking and even pranks of the kind we pulled have changed. No doubt some of the things we did during those two glorious years at Macdonald would get you serious jail time today.

At the first sign of snow, Peter Haydon showed up on campus with a full-length, black overcoat, the bottom fringe of which swept the ground. He never took it off even in class. He probably would have slept in that coat, had it not been for the fact that when glass breaks against your skin it can do some serious damage. Pete was not into damaging himself, believe me.

It was Neil Sorely who started calling him "Portable Pete," in recognition of his delightful genius.

"Like a drink?" Pete would ask and flip open the left side of his overcoat. There, stitched into the lining, were several rows of pockets just large enough to contain a small bottle of pretty well whatever kind of booze suited your fancy. Before you had a chance to get your wits in order, he'd flip open the other flap. "Like a glass with that?" The fee, as I recall, was 50 cents a shot, but you had to return the glass!

Fortunately, Pete wasn't wearing his "like a drink?" coat when the Brockville police hauled us off to jail in the belief we were the desperate characters we looked like.

Not having slept or bathed much to speak of in three days, sporting two and in some cases three days of facial rubble, no doubt we looked like pretty desperate characters indeed. The fact that we had all been popping something called "No Doze" pills (guaranteed to prevent sleep or your money back) didn't help much either.

I want you to know there was nothing illegal about those pills. We didn't take them to get high or anything, we just didn't want to waste any time sleeping. Today they'd get you banned from the

Olympic Games for life, but in those days you could buy them in any truck stop. They kept you awake all right, but the side effects made your eyes bug out, your limbs twitch and your speech slur. Any self-respecting cop would have done exactly what they did in Brockville. Pull out the riot guns, call in backup, surround us, then hustle us to the nearest jail.

We five "desperadoes" were returning from a foolhardy trip to the Guelph Royal. Going was such a spur-of-the-moment decision that we didn't bother bringing a change of underwear, let alone a razor. Pete just announced after a forestry class one day that he was "blowing this pop stand for the Guelph Royal," and if anyone wanted to come, "get your bum into gear 'cause there's a '54 Ford leaving right about now!"

The Guelph Royal was an annual affair similar to one held at Macdonald during which students got a chance to prepare and show various animals in the ring. Very educational! That's what we told our parents. In reality, it was a wonderful excuse to party, and word was making the rounds that no one partied like the girls of Guelph. The only girl Pete ever looked at was the one in the picture he carried around in his wallet. (The one he later married.) The rest of us, however, were not averse to checking out some foreign territory!

As you might imagine, the whole thing is more or less a giant blur from the time I took the first "No Doze" until the sound of sirens. The flashing lights cleared some of the brain dust, as well. The early morning light was just filtering through the mist drifting up from the St. Lawrence when it happened. The Holsteins (that's what we called black and white police cruisers) sported the Brockville logo, so we knew where we were. Now all we needed to know was what we had done!

One Holstein pulled in front of us; another almost put his front bumper through our trunk. Pete seemed a little dazed. "Geez, Pete, pull over. What the hell have you done?" yelled Neil. For once Pete didn't argue. Gingerly he applied the brake, fearful that the cruiser up our backside was going to do serious damage to his mother's car. When we finally stopped, a third cruiser came careening around the corner, sirens blaring, lit up like a Christmas tree.

We sat stunned as an army of cops poured out, some armed with what looked like small cannons. I'd watched plenty of cop movies. "Whatever you do," I said, "don't anybody make any sudden moves." Out of the corner of his mouth, Pete said, "Lushwell, that's probably the smartest idea you've ever had!"

George Duncan, who today operates a sawmill in the lovely little community of Macdonald's Corners, still claims he wasn't the least bit worried. Maybe so, but I was scared silly, especially when they jammed everyone, except Pete, into one small cell and slammed the door shut. Neil, only half joking, wondered aloud if they had taken Pete out to torture him.

They weren't torturing him. What they were trying to do was find out if he was telling the truth. His claim that he was Senator Haydon's grandson, that his brother was a big shot up there in Ottawa and that this was his mother's car wasn't going over too well. The lack of ownership or insurance papers didn't help. A late-model blue Ford just like ours had been stolen after a break-in and we looked very much like the break-in type. As luck would have it, Pete's mother wasn't at home to verify Pete's assertions, nor could his brother be tracked down. Meantime, back in the cell, we four tried stretching out on the floor, but we'd had so much "No Doze" that our legs started twitching and our bugged-out eyes wouldn't shut.

It was at least noon when we finally got things straightened out and the disappointed Brockville police scraped open the cell door. If memory serves me right, Pete's car mysteriously disappeared shortly after that. When asked, Pete would only mumble something about mothers and unauthorized trips.

It was the bowling ball episode that solidified Peter Haydon's status as a full-blown semi-legendary character. Don't ask me where he got it, but Pete showed up one day with a bowling ball. Not the little five-pin wimpy ball, but the big jobbie with the finger holes and all. The kind you've seen Ralphie carry on reruns of "The Honeymooners." There were no house rules against bowling balls, but when they caught Pete converting one of the hallways into a bowling alley with beer cans as pins, it was game over.

"Once too often, Mr. Haydon," harrumphed the authorities. "When we caught you removing the shower heads, we warned you that one more episode and you were out of residence. By the way, take your bowling ball with you." Authorities everywhere, as you know, have absolutely no sense of humour!

At Macdonald they still talk about the mock funeral we held for poor old Pete. At every class reunion, we pull out a picture and laugh all over again. There's Neil decked out in a huge black parson's hat, leading the solemn-faced procession. The coffin is a little small, but then, as someone said, so was Pete. I'm carrying a large sign that says: "Herein lies the Spirit of Peter Scott Haydon, R.I.P." The entire class, heads bowed, is strung out behind. As we wind our way through the giant dining room, someone begins to pound out a slow rhythmic beat on a table. The entire room picks it up. A hundred giant tom-toms! We fall into step. It's a wonderful effect. Very moving. Too bad poor old Pete couldn't be there to see it.

We didn't see much of Pete after that. He moved into a nearby apartment, attended some classes, but seemed subdued. Not the same old Pete at all. We missed him terribly.

We still miss him. Pete succumbed to leukemia several years ago. Our classmates dwindle down to a precious few. Last year, I spotted a full bottle of Red Cap beer for sale at an antique auction. It occupies a place of honour in our house

Here's to you, Portable Pete!

. . .

Dew Worms and Sudden Death

The way I got into radio is one of those crazy things for which there is just no explanation. It was mostly thanks to dew worms and just plain and simple good luck!

I'm not afraid to admit it. When I graduated from Macdonald College in the spring of 1956, I was not a happy camper, as they say today. I had really nowhere to go. Portable Pete, Neil, Milt, George and all the rest of my friends had gone home. The great romance that had occupied me for almost a year at Macdonald was over and the only job available was milking cows and cleaning stables. A few days of that at a Jersey farm near Hudson, Quebec, with a nutcase farm manager convinced me there had to be something better to do with my life.

They were running TV adds urging all bright young guys to go soaring off into the wild blue yonder with the RCAF, so I said to myself, hey, what the heck, I'd look pretty good jockeying one of those things around; I think I'll become a jet pilot!

And I almost did. I took all the brain and muscle power tests they could throw at me and passed with flying colours. "You're in!" they told me, there's just one minor problem. The actual pilot training at that time was done in London, Ontario. Problem was they needed several students per class, so I would have to wait until they found a few more perfect prospects.

Against my better judgement, I was boarding with my mother

and her new husband, Bert Whetter, in Brantford at the time, so the RCAF sprang for an open-ended one-way bus ticket from Brantford to London. When they had sufficient students to form a class they would phone me. All I had to do then was hop on a bus, get myself to London and my life was pretty well set.

I had no idea how long it would take to round up the required classmates, so I moseyed into the Brantford Unemployment Office and inquired about some work to fill in the days until the big call-up.

They sat me down with a strange-looking little guy who, when learning of my diploma in agriculture, decided we had something in common. Shyly, he broke the news. He raised dew worms as a hobby! Dew worms! I didn't burst out laughing or even suggest I'd never heard of such a thing, which was pure blind luck since I wasn't all that well-equipped with common sense or diplomacy in those days.

Having spent countless nights as a kid crawling around on my hands and knees through dew-laden grass catching night crawlers (really big dew worms) to sell to fishermen, I was even able to share a couple of dew worm disaster stories. (I once put a week's catch in the freezer instead of the fridge.)

This guy (I sure wish I could recall his name) was obviously pretty impressed with locating a kindred spirit, because he dug into his desk and pulled out a sheet of paper. "You know," he said, "CKPC is looking for a legman; you should go down there and see them."

I was puzzled. "What's CKPC?" "The local radio station," he said. "It's down the other end of Colborne Street. You sound pretty bright; why don't you go down and talk with a guy by the name of Al Chandler. He's the news director." My next question seemed pretty reasonable to me. "What's a legman?" "Some kind of junior reporter," he said, someone they can send out to cover things like city council meetings, fires, stuff like that." I thanked him, took the address and left, convinced this guy was nuts. I knew nothing about radio, nothing about city councils, nothing about reporting. As Grandpa Green would have said, I knew plenty of nothin' about nothin'!

But the more I thought about it, the more intrigued I became. So I walked the few blocks to the big old house that in those days housed the only radio station in Brantford, met Al Chandler, and was hired on the spot. Forty-five bucks a week, including Saturdays, and no one kept track of hours. Which meant, I quickly learned, that on average you were working from about 6 a.m. until 11 p.m.

I would gladly have worked 24 hours a day. It was by far the most exciting thing I had ever done. I fell in love with radio, a love that has never slackened. Radio still is to me by far the most exciting thing anyone could ever do. Thank heavens for dew worms!

A few weeks later I got a phone call from the RCAF informing me that my pilot's training course would begin in a few days in London and I should use that bus ticket. I never did get on that bus. I still have the ticket someplace. If I ever tire of broadcasting, who knows, I may use it.

• • •

Without Al Chandler, I would never have survived as a legman, or anything else in radio. He took me under his wing and treated me almost as a son. I had no way of knowing it, but Al was a legend in the news business. Not just in radio. He was also a correspondent and photographer for the now-defunct *Toronto Telegram* and would stop at nothing to get a story.

He sported one of those pushed-back-off-the-forehead fedoras newsmen always wore in old movies, and had always at the ready one of those huge Crown Graphic cameras (the kind you also see in old movies). I quickly learned that not only was I working for CKPC, but for Al Chandler and the *Telegram*. It was only CKPC that paid me, however! No problem. I loved it all! Bring it on!

Except once.

It was Al who called. "Lowell, get out to Park Road with a camera. A hydro lineman has been electrocuted." I did as I was told, but I was very apprehensive. My stepfather Bert was a lineman with Brantford Hydro, and I knew many of his fellow workers. There was a small crowd gathered around the foot of a hydro pole when I arrived. I immediately spotted Bert's best friend, "Shorty." One look at him and I knew. "Who is it, Shorty?" I asked, fearing the worst. It must have been shock, that made him reply, "You'll have to see for yourself."

It was Bert. Killed instantly when he touched a high-voltage "live" wire atop a pole he was doing repair work on. The kind of work he had done for years. Incredible! Here was a guy who survived the entire Italian campaign and the liberation of Holland. He had landed with Canadian forces on Sicily, battled through horrendous mud and rain up through the boot of Italy, taken part in the vicious battle of Ortona, then been shipped to Europe to take part in the liberation of Holland. Done it all without a scratch! Now he lay dead at the foot of a hydro pole.

I was supposed to come back with the story and pictures but could not. It was I who had to break the news to my mother and my half-brother Paul, who fortunately was too young to really under-stand. It was one of the most difficult things I have ever had to do. Al Chandler was like a father to me during those dark days. Sadly, as often happens with young men, I was in too much of a hurry to properly thank him. I wish he were still alive so he could read this.

I had gone to high school in Brantford with Al Chandler's

nephew, Lenny (Pudge) Chandler who, although only about five foot four or five and weighing not much more than 150 pounds, was determined to play professional football. Sheer determination brought Pudge to the CFL, where he played for both the Toronto Argonauts and the Ottawa Rough Riders.

Al was probably shorter then Pudge but I am sure outweighed him by at least 20 or 30 pounds. Al Chandler was about as close to being square in shape as a human could be. Put another 100 pounds around his middle and you would have a perfect sumo wrestler. His fingers were so short and stubby he had great difficulty typing—each finger more or less took up two keys! He had a funny high-pitched voice and laugh and was a wild man with a razor blade.

By the time I arrived each morning at the station, Al would already have a foot-high pile of newspaper clippings teetering on my desk. Scattered thither and yon throughout the building would be shreds of various newspapers that he had attacked with his razor blade, carving out huge chunks.

Al wanted nothing but local news. It was his theory that almost every story around the world had some kind of local angle. "Get the local angle," was his constant mantra. Thus it was that CKPC listeners would hear: *Brantford firemen were anxious last night as two Yonge Street buildings in Toronto went up in flames.* Or: *Brantford police are on the alert the for two daring bank robbers who struck the Bank of Montreal in downtown Vancouver last night.*

Attention spans must have been longer in those days. I recall writing stories about city council meetings which took Charlie Doering three or four minutes to read—as long as the average entire radio newscast today!

Actually, if it hadn't been for Charlie Doering, I might still be frozen to my typewriter. That first morning on the job, Al had headed out to cover something, leaving me his huge pile of clippings. I was sitting there at the typewriter, paralyzed with fear, when Charlie came bursting into the newsroom. "What's the problem?" he asked. "Geez, Charlie, I never wrote a news story in my life, what the hell do I do here? How do I write this?" Charlie gave me the best advice I ever had. "Just start writing. Put something down on the paper. Just start writing!" I did and I still am.

Charlie was one of the great guys in the radio business. I ran across him many years later at CFRB. He was about to retire from broadcasting a daily feature and recommended that I take it over. "Lowell," he told me, "you sound great, you sound really great!" He was the only one at CFRB ever to say it, even though to tell the honest to God's truth, I did sound great!

The big star on CKPC in those days was another really great guy, Bill Brady, and his imaginary sidekick, Murgatroid. One late night as I poured over my city council notes, a drunk staggered into the building demanding to see Murgatroid. "I'm going to punch that little son of a bitch out," he said. "He's making jokes about Newfies again."

I tried to convince him that Murgatroid was not a real person. "He's just a figment of Bill Brady's imagination," I told him. That stopped him. "What do you mean a figment? What's a figment? Where is that little son of a bitch?" I had a brainwave. This guy was too easy. "Listen," I said. "A figment means that Bill Brady has a very serious mental problem. He's not responsible for what he says." The drunk blinked a couple times. I saddened my voice. "To tell the truth, the figment is so serious Bill probably doesn't have much longer to live and he's got five kids you know." By the time I was finished, the drunk was sobbing and apologizing all over the place. "Tell him he can make all the jokes about Newfies he wants," sniffled the guy. "It's okay, geez!"

I told Bill the story the next morning. He laughed himself silly and made a point of having Murgatroid crack at least one Newfie joke every morning for the next week. Bill went on to bigger and better things in London, becoming one of that city's most loved and respected citizens.

I don't want you to get the idea that everybody in the broadcast business is a candidate for sweetheart of the month. I was greeted one morning in the newsroom by a guy who looked like he'd slept in a ditch. He sported a yellowed, tattered, dirty nylon shirt with some kind of green coloured pants whose knees were coated with mud, and torn running shoes but no socks. A cloud of alcohol fumes floated over a head whose hair had apparently not been combed or washed for days.

I thought another bum had wandered in off the street and was about to throw him out when he stuck out his hand. "How ya doing?" Here he gave his name which I won't give to you in case this guy is still alive and has cleaned up his act. (If he is still alive he most certainly must have cleaned up his act!) "Got my newscast ready?" I was stunned. He had a broad friendly smile and one of the most beautiful voices I had ever heard.

If you had turned CKPC on that day and listened to the 8 a.m. news, you would probably have checked your dial to make sure you hadn't accidentally tuned into WABC in New York. The guy was that good!

Fortunately, you would not have seen what was going on. As he read the news, "the voice," as I immediately dubbed him, was holding a small cooking pot filled with chicken noodle soup. Several long strands of noodles had spilled down his chin and dribbled onto his shirt.

After three or four items, he had a brief break while someone else read the sports and weather. Here he tipped the pot back and proceeded to gulp down the entire can of Campbell's best. I was standing in the control room, watching with amazement this performance on the other side of the glass. He smacked his lips, retrieved a noodle from his shirt and, with that big smile of his, pushed the "talk-back" button. "How do I sound?" I gave him the big thumbs up. He sounded wonderful. He just looked like something that had dropped out of the rear end of a tall cow!

This performance was repeated each morning for as long as he stayed with us.

We had a little lunchroom with a hot plate at the rear of our small newsroom. Each morning "the voice" would stagger in with a can of Campbell's Chicken Noodle Soup, which he had undoubtedly picked up at Joe Pinchero's College Fruit Market just up the street. He'd fumble around until he managed to open the can, pour it into the pot, which got filthier each morning, let it warm up a bit, then take it with him into the studio to read the news.

Each morning it was the same thing. Read some news, sock back some soup, then ask, "How do I sound?" The amazing thing was that he was so drunk some mornings we could barely understand him off-air, but when he punched that mike on... Wow!

Another person who had that same amazing ability to sober up when the mike was on was Farley Mowat. Farley, of course, is one of Canada's most outstanding authors and far from a bum, but when he used to appear on my show, he did love his rum! I'd usually get the phone call in the morning. "Green—Mowat. I'm on your show today. I need the usual."

It didn't matter if I had lined up Prestor John, John the Baptist, King Lear and the Pope for my show that afternoon, they all had to be cancelled to make way for Farley Mowat. The "usual" was a bottle of his favourite rum and a large pitcher of ice water.

During the course of a two-hour show, Farley would down the whole thing, scaring the bejabbers out of me in the process.

As the show progressed and the rum disappeared, Farley would get more and more out of control, but only when the mike was turned off. He'd say things I don't wish to tell you, sometimes laughing, sometimes not, during commercials and newscasts. I'd warn him. "Farley, for God sakes, you can't say that on the air!" I think he was play-acting a bit, because when I punched that mike on, only the keenest listener would suspect that Farley was into his cups a bit.

There was one thing that did give him away. When the rum was down to about an inch from the bottom, Farley would start to get a little amorous with the ladies who called. It didn't matter if it sounded like your 95-year-old maiden aunt or a 12-year-old school girl, Farley would start calling them dear and dropping hints that he was a little lonely visiting here in Ottawa.

He was a wonderful guest, full of wit and wisdom, but I must tell you he made me sweat. When we were finished the show, I could have used some of that rum!

My father used to tell a story about Farley Mowat, which he swore was true. Farley had just completed his book *The Boat That Wouldn't Float* and was having difficulty negotiating a publishing deal with Jack McClelland of McClelland & Stewart, Canada's largest publishing house at the time. Things were getting a little dicey between the two. Farley was not happy at all with the offer being made by Jack.

Finally, Farley decided enough was enough. "Look, Jack," he said. "You're going to have to come out here to Newfoundland yourself to get this resolved before some bad blood settles in." So Jack McClelland packed his bags and headed east.

But even face to face they couldn't agree on terms, so Farley suggested they take a little cruise in the boat he had written about. "It's okay, Jack," said Farley, "she floats now!" And so out they went into the Atlantic.

It was a windy day (what day in Newfoundland isn't?), the seas were rough, the boat began to bounce, Jack began to get queasy. "Geez, Farley, let's get back to shore before I puke my guts out." Farley looked at him with scorn. "Jack, we'll head back to shore when you sign this deal here and by the way I brought a pen!" Jack, who was in no condition to argue, said later he had no idea what he was signing. He would have agreed to anything.

Unlike Farley Mowat who remains a Canadian icon, "the voice" disappeared from our lives at CKPC one day. I have no idea where he went or what happened to him. One of the greatest talents I have ever met destroyed by booze. A tragedy really, but sadly not unusual in the broadcast industry.

One of the most popular sportscasters Ottawa ever had got his start thanks to booze. I wasn't at the arena when it happened, but as luck would have it, I was the newsman back in the CKSO-TV Sudbury studios whose brainwave got Hub Beaudry started on the path to broadcast glory.

In those days our radio division carried live broadcasts of Sudbury Wolves Junior A hockey. I forget who they were playing that night, but since this was 1957, it sure wasn't Ottawa which didn't hit the ice for another 10 years.

Our play-by-play man, as was his frequent custom, got drunker and drunker as the game progressed, until by the end of the second period he was completely incoherent. The kid doing colour commentary panicked, called the station and got me. "What the hell do I do here? I need some help. I don't know half the players."

Forget the fact our colour guy doesn't know half the players, I mean this is Sudbury, right! Desperate measures are required. That's when the brainwave hits. "Can you get anyone from the Wolves to help you with the names? See if they can spare a coach." There's a pause at the other end of the line as the panic-stricken guy peers down to the players' bench. In a minute he's back. "There's a guy sitting down there with a cast on his arm. It must be Hub Beaudry. He's a former player who broke his wrist a couple of weeks ago."

The third period was about to start. "If I were you," I said, "I'd get him up there in the booth with you fast. Bluff your way through the play-by-play as best you can and get Hub up there to help you with the names and some colour." That's exactly what happened.

It was probably one of the worst play-by-play calls of any sport in the history of broadcasting, but that's how Hub Beaudry, who became one of Ottawa's most popular sportscasters with the CBC, got his start. Don't ask me what happened to the play-by-play drunk or the colour guy. I can't even remember their names! Hub died in late 2004. It's true what they say: The good *do* die young.

What an adventure that year was with CKSO-TV! Forget the year, how about my welcome? I'd been a year with CKPC, I wanted to get into television, so I said goodbye to Al, Bill and Charlie, threw everything I owned into the back seat of my brand new '56 Meteor and headed north young man. North to the big time: Sudbury!

Believe it or not, CKSO in Sudbury was the first privately owned television station in Canada. In 1957, the rest of television was a CBC monopoly, and unless you spoke with a strong British accent or were gay, your chances of getting air work with the CBC were just about nil. Thus it was that for many of us trying to break into television, including by the way Alex Trebek of "Jeopardy" fame, Sudbury became a magnet.

If you've ever seen one of those cult grade "B" movies of

spacemen on the moon or Mars, you have a pretty good idea what Sudbury looked like in 1957. As a matter of fact, if you saw one of those movies, you may very well have seen Sudbury. It was not at all unusual to see a movie crew out on the rocks shooting scenes depicting the face of the moon or Pluto or some distant planet whose inhabitants were about to attack earth.

Bare black rocks were all there was to see in Sudbury in those days. The noxious fumes pouring from the nickel smelters' smokestacks killed everything resembling grass or trees for miles around. Moss made a few valiant attempts at sprouting on the rocks most distant from the smokestacks, but a day or two after a wind shift the dull green turned to dull grey and blew away like ash. I once did a feature about a guy who painted the rock in his front yard solid green. "Grass without the lawn mower," he explained.

. . .

Sudbury Saturday Night

I am trying to shake off the fatigue of an all-night drive in the dull grey November dawn as I crest a hill and come face to face with horror! A light skiff of snow dusts across bleak, black, bare rock to my right. To my left, wind whips a dusting of snow across bleak, black, bare rock. The picture in front is exactly the same: snow skittering back and forth across bleak, black, bare rock. Hell itself could not be as hopelessly barren.

If I'd had a full tank of gas or some money in my pocket, I would have yanked that '56 Meteor around in a full U-turn right then and there and made a run for it. But with a nearly empty wallet and gas tank and a totally empty heart, I had no choice.

It is on to Sudbury just over that next barren pile of rocks and drifting snow…or starvation! Besides which, I tell myself, I can stick it out at least a week in this godforsaken place, then escape with a paycheque.

It must have been culture-shock befuddlement that prevents me from bolting when I check into the Nickel Range Hotel and find there is no door on the room CKSO reserved for me. The desk clerk isn't the least bit apologetic when he calmly explains there had been a fight in the room the night before and the door was ripped off its hinges. "When do you think I'll have a door?" I ask. "Oh, I guess when we can find one that fits."

Stompin' Tom Connors later wrote a song about it: "Sudbury Saturday Night." (Well, it could have been about it.)

First thing Monday morning, I undergo the "intensive" training course CKSO promised. "Here's a movie camera, this here's the button to turn it on. Here's a still camera, everybody knows how to use one of them, and this is your tape recorder. Now here's a map that shows you how to get to Elliot Lake. We'd like a couple stories for the 11 o'clock news tonight. Any questions?"

Of course not! Why would I have any questions?

What they should have equipped me with was a couple of six-shooters and a bulletproof vest. Elliot Lake in 1957 was the biggest, wildest, most dangerous frontier boomtown since the days of the Klondike gold rush.

During the height of the Cold War and the nuclear arms race, uranium and lots of it had been discovered deep in the bush about 100 miles west and north of Sudbury. What could be better than that?

Almost overnight a town is blasted out of the rock, bush and muskeg. Hundreds and then thousands of individuals—miners, farmers, carpenters, engineers, truck drivers, bums, thugs and ladies of the night—pour in from all over Canada, then from all over the world. One day there is a swamp, the next day a shopping centre. Money flows like water.

I once have to pay $50 for a battery charge, half a week's pay. Expensive boutiques do a thriving business. So do the bars and the brothels!

I almost starve that first week. I had poured almost every cent I had into my Meteor's gas tank and coffee and doughnuts on the way up Highway 11 to the frozen north. Coffee and a hamburger in Elliot Lake can't be bought for under $5. Coffee and a doughnut will set you back at least $3. Please don't forget that in those days the $100 a week I was earning was very good pay, indeed, for most Canadians. In Sudbury, however, during the "boom" time, the miners were making double that.

To make matters really bad, I won't get paid until the end of the week. I am staying in a tiny one-room apartment built into the base of our transmitter building. The bathtub is so filthy you have to chip the crud off with a chisel, but whoever lived there before left a five-pound bag of potatoes under the sink. By dint of scrapping off the rotten portions, I manage to stave off starvation, but just barely.

It's a wonder I can stare a potato in the eye today. And those were the days when I didn't need to go on a diet!

The only thing cheap in Elliot Lake is life itself. Law is almost non-existent. Scarcely a day goes by without a violent death, sometimes several. They die beneath falling rocks in hastily constructed mine shafts. Their arms are severed or legs crushed in machinery operated by those with little or no training. In alcoholic hazes they kill or maim each other, their wives, their friends, and in some cases even their husbands, with axes, shovels and guns. Sometimes with whatever is handy. And always they smash their new high-powered cars into rock cuts that rim the only road leading in and out.

There are so many deaths and injuries that after a while we only bother to report the most spectacular. A single man crushed beneath a falling rock isn't worth mentioning on the news. A dozen perhaps. My story of the father who goes berserk and kills his wife and two children with an axe is lead item on the 11 p.m. news, but the rule is that we only cover car crashes that kill two or more people.

It was wild, it was exciting, it was like nothing this country has ever seen or will see again. I wouldn't have missed it for the world, but after a year I figured it was time to get out of there while I was still alive. Time for the really big time: Woodstock!

. . .

The Crab Monster!

What do you think of a radio station where the chief engineer (the *only* engineer) is named Peter Rabbits, and his chief means of getting us onto the air is to administer a swift kick to the equipment? Pretty primitive, eh? That station is CKOX, Woodstock, in the summer of 1958. The first station where I am certain I have terminated my own career.

After about a year of counting bodies at Elliot Lake, I clue in to the fact that the people making the really big bucks in broadcasting and getting all the glory (and the girls) are the on-air people. I'm right "up there" as a reporter and writer, but if I want to make it in the big time I have to get in front of a microphone or camera.

So here I am at CKOX in Woodstock, which from time to time, when Peter Rabbits kicks the equipment in the right place, we actually get onto the air. I read everything from sports to farm features to news and commercials. I begin to suspect I am the only broadcaster they have. And I'm not actually a broadcaster!

There is nothing, I assure you, more nerve-wracking than those first few weeks on-air. You are so nervous you actually shake. One of the big problems is sucking in enough air to keep your heart beating. This is true even if your audience, as in Woodstock, totals probably only a few hundred. A few hundred, a few hundred thousand…the sheer terror of it is the same!

The shakes have calmed to about a 6 on the Richter scale when, in the middle of a half-hour news and sportscast, I have to read a commercial for the local drive-in movie theatre. You won't remember the movie. No one will except me. It is an early version of that cult favourite *Attack of the Killer Tomatoes,* only this one is called *Attack of the Crab Monsters.*

Halfway through the commercial, I make a terrible mistake. I glance up into the control room and there on the other side of the glass is Peter Rabbits pretending to rip his crotch to shreds! I look down trying to stifle a snicker, but I have lost my place so have to start over again. I can't resist. I am drawn to the spectacle like some kind of fatal magnet. He's still there, still at it, Peter Rabbits clawing at his crotch.

What happens next is not a pretty sight and it certainly isn't a pretty sound. A few lines of news, a stifled giggle, then loud shrieks of laughter. Over and over again for a full 15 minutes. I can't stop. White-faced station owner Monty Wherry charges into the control room and the crotch attack is arrested in mid-scratch, but not the insane performance in the studio. I am out of control.

And do you know the scariest thing about all of this? The station doesn't receive a single phone call, either of complaint or concern. Monty threatens both Peter Rabbits and I with some terrible things, but because Mr. Rabbits is the only one who knows where to kick the equipment and I am his only announcer, we get to keep our jobs.

I, however, decide I can't live in a place where the listeners will accept a performance as bad as mine, so I head for the really big time: Montreal and fame, if not fortune!

• • •

Of Fights and Photos

October 10, 1958—Montreal Forum—Archie Moore vs. Yvon Durelle for the Light Heavyweight Championship of the World. One of the greatest fights in history.

Durelle has Moore down three times in the first round. The partisan crowd goes crazy. We're going to have a Canadian champion. A French Canadian at that! Or so we all believe. If it were today, the fight would probably have been stopped after the third knock-down, but Moore, the cagey old veteran, gets up, goes into a shell for a couple of rounds and holds on. He's dropped by Durelle again in the fourth round, gets up once again on his incredibly spindly legs and somehow knocks Durelle out in the 11th.

I'm there in the front row covering the event for United Press International. The fight was fantastic, but what happened before and after the fight are the things I remember most.

I had the "dressing room" assignment. Do a colour story from Durelle's dressing room prior to the fight, and interview the winner when it's all over, were my orders from UPI sports editor Dick Bacon.

With press credentials, I have no problem getting into Durelle's dressing room; getting him to comment is another story. I struck out completely with the interview attempt, as did all other reporters, but the story I did write was carried in newspapers around the world.

Believe it or not, Yvon Durelle was unavailable for pre-fight interviews because he was down on his knees in a corner with a couple of trainers rolling dice! Minutes before he was going into the ring for the Light Heavyweight Championship of the World with its fame and fortune, Yvon Durelle is down on a dirty cement floor playing craps for a few dollars!

Since Archie Moore won, it was my job after the fight to paint a word picture of the scene in his dressing room. As you can imagine, it was a madhouse. It was a dank and dingy place, somewhere deep in the bowels of the Forum, jammed with handlers, trainers, hangers-on, reporters and photographers. Shouted questions, excited laughter; the stink of sweat, rosin and blood (Archie's).

I have been told Archie is a gentleman and will answer any reasonable question. Even though in obvious pain, he is sitting on a training table, smiling, nodding and doing his best to answer the questions being fired at him from every direction.

Among the photographers jammed in with us is a female version of Al Chandler. Built like a fire plug, legs at least twice as thick as Archie's, a face that looked like it had gone a few rounds with him. From one of the New York papers I am told, although I never did get her name.

She has rounded up a chair and is standing on it in the corner yelling in a distinct Bronx accent, "*Awh-chee*, look up *he-ya*." Moore pays no attention. Louder this time: "Moore, look up *he-ya*." Archie either doesn't hear or chooses to ignore her. A third attempt, loud enough for us all to hear, including I am certain Archie: "*Awh-chee*, damn it, look up *he-ya* at momma." This gets a chuckle from a few of us, but Moore still refuses to pay attention.

Then a bullhorn voice: "Moore, look up *he-ya*, damn it, or I'll come down there and kick the shit out of you!" She gets her picture—a huge ear to ear grin.

• • •

The "Bump"

In Springhill, Nova Scotia, as in Montreal, we are having a beautiful Indian-summer day. October 23 is late to be having temperatures well into the 70s which makes it all the more welcome, especially after all the rain the fall of 1958 had dumped on us.

In Springhill, 174 men are more than a mile beneath the Atlantic Ocean, mining the rich bituminous coal seam in the Cumberland Rail and Coal company's No. 2 mine.

In Montreal, I am finishing my shift at United Press International (UPI), a major wire service conglomerate supplying news and features to newspapers and radio stations around the world. As features editor, I write a couple of features a day on agriculture and music, but for the most part my job is to select major stories pouring into our office from a dozen other wire services (Teletype machines) and rewrite them for our radio service.

My shift ends at 8 p.m., but my replacement is late. I'm the rookie, so I've got to wait until he shows up.

At 8:12, the "bulletin bells" on the Canadian Press wire service begin to ring. I'm not too excited. Canadian Press has been known to bulletin some remarkably mundane things, including reported sightings of UFOs.

They got it right this time. What confronts me is the world's first notice of one of the most dramatic and tragic stories of the twentieth century.

I remember it, as if it were yesterday:

Oct. 23-8:12p (CP)——Halifax-Flash——Explosion—— Springhill, NS Cumberland Co #2 mine. 174 trapped——more

My immediate job is to transfer that "Flash" to the UPI news wires feeding into several hundred newspapers around the world and onto the UPI service used by Canadian radio stations.

I am processing the subsequent flashes, bulletins and follow-up stories that flood the wires shortly after midnight when Tommy McQuaid, UPI's Montreal news director calls to say I am to immediately get to Dorval Airport. An airplane chartered by Cumberland Rail and Coal flying journalists from Toronto and Montreal to Springhill will pick me up within the hour.

No. 2 mine was one of the richest and deepest coal mines in the world. It slanted 14,600 feet down under the Atlantic Ocean and reached at its greatest vertical depth 4,350 feet.

As the 3 p.m. shift descended, the trolley cars (called rakes) disgorged groups of men at various levels—some at 13,000, others at 13,400, and the final group at the 13,800-foot level.

It wasn't an explosion that ripped through No. 2 mine this time, as had occurred twice before, killing 125 in 1891 and 39 in 1956. Tonight it was what miners fear even more: a "bump."

Bumps usually occur only in very deep mines, the result of changing pressure. They are, in effect, small earthquakes, shaking the subterranean shafts with incredible force. This bump smashed along a working seam of coal from the 12,600-foot level down to the 13,800-foot level. In some cases, the mine floor was jammed up against the ceiling. Many men died instantly. Steel rails and foot-thick bracing timbers were hurled aside like matchsticks.

Above ground, every building in Springhill shook. The shock was registered on a university seismograph in Halifax, 70 miles away. It hit at precisely five minutes past eight, just as Springhill Mayor Ralph Gilroy was opening the town council meeting.

Mayor Gilroy and his five council members dashed for the door and ran towards the mine entrance at the edge of town. So did almost every resident. There were very few in Springhill who did not have a husband, son, brother or uncle underground.

One of them was veteran miner Gorley Kempt. He was

walking up to the wall near the junction of the 13,000-foot level to repair a coal conveyor pan. Here's how he described to me what happened: "Suddenly the pavement seemed to explode. Everything flew with a terrible rushing noise and wind."

Another man underground when the bump hit was 38-year-old Joe McDonald, who had been injured in the 1956 explosion. He told me, "I was bent over digging coal with a pick. Suddenly the face of coal came toward me and the floor jumped seven feet." Joe landed with a coal pan on top of him. His leg was broken in three places. He swung his lamp and saw a solid wall of coal and rock where seven men had been at work. He screamed.

Wilfred Hunter never heard a sound. He was working alongside his brother Frank when he found himself spitting coal, trying to push a large rock off his legs. In total darkness, he groped around and felt a body wedged into the rock over his head. He was certain it was his brother.

When the other reporters and I arrived in Springhill early next morning, 80 men had been rescued. Ninety-four were still down there somewhere.

It was a sight I will never forget. It had started to rain lightly. The mine entrance was roped off. Just behind it stood a crowd of townspeople, some silent, some softly weeping, some praying. We were told that draegermen (miners especially trained for rescue work) were on their way, driving from other Nova Scotia mines. Some, in fact, had already assisted in rescue operations overnight.

The search for survivors was incredibly difficult and dangerous. Electrical equipment could not be used for fear of triggering a gas explosion. Methane gas had been released by the bump at several levels. Men, covered in black soot, worked on their bellies and knees with sawed-off shovels, picks and their bare hands.

Dislodged coal and rock often had to be dumped into a pail, then passed back from man to man in narrow passageways being cleared. In one eight-hour shift, the rescuers were able to advance less than ten feet. Always was the danger of another bump. The mine continued to shake from time to time from aftershocks. No one paid any attention. There was a job to be done.

The bump occurred Thursday evening. We arrived early Friday morning. At noon Friday, there were tears in my eyes as I wrote that Harold Gordon, general manager of coal operations for Cumberland's parent firm, Dominion Steel and Coal Corp., announced, "There is little hope for more survivors." Ninety-four men were still missing.

"Gordon was crying openly when he made the announcement," I wrote, "but the rain-drenched crowd at the pit remained steadfast." Mayor Gilroy said simply, "We've got to pray." The rescue operations continued unabated. Prince Phillip arrived with a minimum of fanfare and quietly urged that hope not be abandoned. There were similar messages from around the world, including one from the Pope.

In the homes of the missing miners, sentiment ranged from wavering hope to utter despair. Margaret Guthro, whose husband Hugh had not been found, told me that by Monday, "I was sure Hughie wouldn't come out alive. I told the children to prepare for the fact he was dead. I made funeral arrangements and even moved some of the furniture out of the living room to make way for his coffin." She was not alone. Several other wives began making similar arrangements.

At the other end of the spectrum was Marguerite Kempt. "I had a feeling Gorley was all right," she told me. She kept the house lights burning through each night because she told me, "It just didn't feel right to turn them out when you are expecting someone to come home."

I cannot adequately describe to you the joy we all felt when early Wednesday evening the news tore through town that voices from some of the trapped men had been heard at the end of an air tube.

Twelve are still alive said the voice of Gorley Kempt, "For God sakes, we need water." We learned later that the men were so desperate for water that they had begun drinking their own urine, filtering it through coal dust first. At six o'clock Wednesday evening, October 29, 1958, six days after the bump, a copper tube slid down the ventilation pipe. Water poured through. "Caleb, say grace for us," said Hugh Guthro. Rushton held his water can and said, "Oh Lord, we thank you for the pipe and the blessed water."

They settled down then to await rescue, praying that another bump would not strike. The entire town was there at the pit head shortly before 3 a.m. Thursday when 12 men—their eyes covered with blankets to protect them from the light—were carried on stretchers out of the shaft and into waiting ambulances. Unable to see, Joe McDonald asked what the noise was all about. "People are cheering you," said one of the draegermen. "That's good," said Joe, "I thought it was the bill collectors waiting for us."

By Friday noon, most of the reporters from around the world had left, convinced that no one could still be alive after more than a week buried in the mine with no food or water.

My reports had begun to appear in leading newspapers around the world. In particular, there had been several front-page stories in the *New York Times* under my byline, so UPI asked that I remain for at least another day and provide some wrap-up coverage.

Late Friday night, I wrote what I thought was my last story and caught a cab to Moncton, New Brunswick, where a flight was scheduled to leave for Montreal the next morning.

During my week in Springhill, I had befriended a young man whose uncle was one of those killed in the bump. Shortly after

4 o'clock the next morning, I was awakened in my hotel room by the telephone. It was my young friend. "They've found seven more," he said and started to cry.

Thus it was that I was the first to report to the world news of another miracle in Springhill. I immediately phoned UPI back in Montreal. "Bulletin it," I said. "They've found seven more. I'm heading back right now and will file the full story as soon as I get there."

Reporters began rushing back to Springhill that Saturday morning, but I was the only international news agency source at the site for several hours, and most of what the world read and heard about the miraculous rescue of seven more men came from my typewriter.

The rescue was the first of two miracles I reported that day. For more than six days before being rescued, a badly injured Wilfred Hunter lay trapped in total darkness believing that the body he could feel pinned to the roof above him was that of his brother Frank. Of the final seven men rescued three days later, one was Frank Hunter.

It was the last of the miracles. Seventy-five men died. The mine was closed forever and Springhill ceased to be a mining town.

When I get back to Montreal, I get a handshake from Tommy McQuaid and a $50 bonus.

· · ·

Hello Folks!

Given my past, rather sorry, experience with banks, I am getting one big kick out of this! I've just handed a clerk at the Somerset and Bank branch of the Bank of Nova Scotia in downtown Ottawa a cheque made out to me from CFRA Radio for $40,000. I ask to use it to open a new account in my name.

Imagine walking into a strange bank today and proffering a check for half a million dollars. Because in 1960 when a good salary was $5,000 a year, comparatively speaking that's roughly what we're talking about.

The teller takes one look at the cheque and turns pale. The news that something strange is up flies around the bank. Customers pause to stare. What is this guy up to? Should we worry?

The clerk mumbles something about waiting a minute and disappears with the cheque. Moments later out from an office comes a fussy little man gingerly holding the cheque as though it is fresh dog poop.

"Do you have some identification, Mr. Green?" I produce my driver's licence. He examines it closely, then peers up at me in obvious deep suspicion. "Do you have an account here?" I shake my head. "No, I would like to open an account with this cheque." He thinks he's onto my game. "You won't be able to withdraw any funds until this cheque clears. That could take a week." He smiles a tight little smile, thinking he's put the kibosh on my scam. "That's fine," I say, then drop the name: "Frank Ryan doesn't believe I will need the money for at least a couple of weeks."

Believe me, you have to be pretty spaced out or downright stupid to live in Ottawa in 1960 and not know who I mean by Frank Ryan.

Our suspicious little man examines the cheque again, paying special attention to the signature which clearly is that of the CFRA president and owner. "I'll have to make a phone call," he says, and then, on the off chance I might be legit, he adds, "Do you mind?" I shake my head no.

He is positively beaming when he returns. The cheque is no

longer dog poop, but $40,000 in real money going to be deposited into his bank. Great day in the morning! He pulls back a bolt, swings open a little wooden door and invites me back behind the counter and into his office where we conclude the transaction. He even asks if I would like a coffee.

When I walk out, I am a rich man. I now have as much money in my personal bank account as I will earn as chief news editor at CFRA for the next seven and a half years! To be perfectly accurate, at my salary of $100 a week (which I almost had to engage in armed combat to get!) I now have as much money in my bank account as I will earn in the next seven years and 36 weeks! Please keep in mind that when I started at CFRA, a week meant six days. Yes, we worked Saturdays.

Sadly, the money will soon be transferred into someone else's bank account, since my job, my very first job at CFRA, is to buy enough land upon which to build a new transmitter site. I am so new at CFRA that no one, except Frank Ryan and his wife Kathleen, know I'm in town. Only they know what I am doing. My mission is top secret!

Frank Ryan is perhaps the shrewdest businessman I have ever met. Just prior to my arrival in the fall of 1960, CFRA had received approval to boost its power from 5,000 to 50,000 watts and change its frequency from 560 to 580 (AM on your dial; FM had yet to be invented). It would greatly increase the station's coverage area, but required a relocation of the transmitter site from the west end of Ottawa to a much larger site south of the Capital.

Frank realized (correctly) that if anyone caught wind that it was he looking for land, the price would skyrocket. Thus my secret mission: Find sufficient land in the correct location and buy it without anyone knowing it is for Frank Ryan and CFRA. "You're from the farm," says Frank, "tell them you're going to raise sheep!"

It wasn't easy. I didn't know Eastern Ontario from Moscow, but I realized that what we were looking for had to be in the Manotick area just a few miles south of our studio in the heart of Ottawa. I finally found a farm that suited us quite well, and managed to buy it at a reasonable price. The problem was we needed another small strip of land for the northernmost tower, and somehow the owner figured out what was going on. Frank Ryan was right. Overnight the price for that narrow strip of land soared from $10,000 to $40,000. Frank ranted and raved for several days. Whether he blamed me for word leaking out I am not sure, but in the end he paid the price and we had our site. The land today, of course, is worth a few million.

It all takes about two months, during which I am a hero at that bank. The manager rushes out each time I walk in and never fails to offer coffee, always inquiring after my health.

The day after the final payment for the land cleans my bank account out to the last penny, I stroll in looking for another free coffee, but the manager after glancing up at me, gets up from his desk and closes his office door. Fame truly is fleeting…and nothing extinguishes it faster than an empty bank account!

The site upon which CFRA's original transmitter was built in 1946 is now an Ottawa subdevelopment called the Ryan Farm, which you probably couldn't buy for a hundred million. Frank bought the whole thing for I believe $25,000, although there is some dispute over the exact amount. What there is no dispute about is the manner in which he made the purchase.

Just as I did several years later, Frank figures where he needs to locate his transmitter towers and sets out to buy sufficient land. He finds his farm at the western edge of Ottawa and offers what most agree is $25,000. The farmer wants $30,000 and won't budge.

1960—Lowell finally hits the big time: CFRA in Ottawa

Yes, it was 560 CFRA when President John F. Kennedy visited Ottawa. News Director Campbell McDonald and Lowell broadcast live from "Uplands Airport."

JFK meets "Dief the Chief" shortly before the President wrenches his back planting a tree at Rideau Hall.

January 1, 1968. "The Flame" lives. Lowell is credited with saving the Centennial Flame which was scheduled to be dismantled at the end of 1967.

It took two hunger strikes on Parliament Hill and several supporting broadcasts by Lowell, but finally Canada's Merchant Navy veterans get their well-deserved pension.

Frank is a very persuasive man and can be incredibly charming. The farmer, however, is adamant. After several hours of fruitless negotiations, Frank suddenly stands up and says, "Look, here's $25,000. I'm going to leave it here. If you decide to take it, give me a call in the morning. If you don't want it, I'll come back, retrieve the money and find another location." At this, he dumps $25,000 in cash in small bills onto the kitchen table and walks out the door.

The farmer and his wife don't sleep a wink that night goes the story, getting up every few minutes to have another look at what $25,000 in cash looks like; what a huge pile it makes heaped there beneath the dangling kitchen light. The phone rings well before seven the next morning at Frank's house. "We'll take it," says the farmer. "I thought you might," replies Frank.

There is an ancient Chinese curse that says: "May you live in interesting times!" I wouldn't go so far as to say working for Frank Ryan was a curse, but it certainly was interesting. As with many visionaries, Frank had a very unpredictable temper and temperament. Mercurial, some would say. Volatile is another word that springs to mind. You were never sure when he would come storming in, flushed with anger, sparks flying off him like Roman candles in the night.

He charged into the Isabella Street studio one early morning around three, furious at something the overnight disc jockey had said, slammed his hand down on a turntable and broke his wrist. Hearing someone in the spring or fall refer to "ground frost" would drive him crazy. "Where else would the frost be?" he'd yell. On the other hand, he understood and appreciated creativity and hard work, and as we learned one day, he could take a joke, even on himself.

Perhaps in response to the new "scruffy" look prompted by that new weird musical group called the Beatles, several CFRA employees began to grow beards. "Watch," said our news director Campbell Macdonald, "this will drive Mr. Ryan around the bend. He won't put up with this for long." Campbell knew Frank Ryan better than most and he called this one exactly right. Two weeks of beards getting shaggier and shaggier was all Frank could take. Up went a big bold notice on the lunch room bulletin board: IT IS STATION POLICY THAT NO MALE EMPLOYEE SHALL WEAR A BEARD. There were several sniggers about female employees and beards, but overnight all facial hair disappeared. Frank was all beaming smiles for a couple days before leaving on a trip.

Or at least Charles Catchpole (radio name Chuck Collins) thought the boss was on a trip.

Chuck shows up in the lunchroom one day with an old moth-eaten fake beard hooked around his ears and dangling down to his belt buckle. You can imagine the hilarity that greets it! Chuck then ambles down the hallway to the elevator, punches the button for the third-floor studios and, whistling away, begins the upward journey.

What's this? The elevator is stopping at the second floor? This can't be. The only office on the second floor is that of Frank Ryan and he's out of the country. The elevator door slides open. There they are—face to face! The magnificently bearded Chuck Collins and Frank Ryan! "I thought I was a goner," Chuck says. "I could see my career, maybe even my life, down the tubes. He stares at me. I stares at him, then suddenly he slaps his knee and breaks into nearly hysterical laughter." "That's great," says Mr. Ryan between guffaws. "That's what we need around here. More creativity. If we had more people like you working here, we'd be number one!" (That was before we *were* number one!)

I had no idea what kind of an institution Frank Ryan was in the Ottawa Valley until I was negotiating the purchase of that Manotick farm for our transmitter site. We are haggling over a difference of $5,000 when suddenly the farmer glances up at the kitchen clock and stops me cold. "We'll have to finish this after Frank," he says and flips on the radio. Exactly 12:30 and there it is, "The Surrey With the Fringe on Top" theme song, followed by the most famous drawl in the Valley: "Hello folks."

It was the same story on every farm from Carleton Place to Calabogie from the time CFRA signed on the air May 3, 1947, until Frank Ryan's death in 1965. If you were farming or had any interest in farming, everything stopped for half an hour to make way for "Farmer's Notebook" and Frank Ryan. Actually when I say half an hour, it could very well be 45 minutes, since when Frank got on a roll, time meant absolutely nothing, and let's face it, if you own the station it is, after all, your time!

Getting Frank onto the air was sometimes as difficult as getting him off. If he wasn't at a fair or in Bermuda, his broadcasts were done from his second-floor office that also served as a studio. The problem was if there was anything confidential to be discussed during the morning, Frank would unplug his microphone and usually forget to plug it back in again.

Each day at 12:30, Campbell Macdonald and I would wait with bated breath in the newsroom as his theme song finished. If we didn't hear his famous "Hello folks," one of us would rush down the stairs, barge into his office, grab the microphone plug and ram it into the wall socket.

Frank never seemed to understand that his audience had missed his first few remarks, because he would continue on as though nothing had happened, only glancing up in minor puzzlement as we plunged into his office. We mentioned the unplugged mike several times to him, but he would only nod distractedly, mumble something and probably leave it unplugged the next day. After a time, Campbell and I seemed able to sense when the mike wasn't plugged in during the theme song and usually managed to make it in time for at least "folks."

• • •

Campbell Macdonald was one of the most buoyant, optimistic men you could hope to find in the kind of pressure cooker that was CFRA with Frank Ryan at the helm. The only time I ever saw Campbell really disturbed about anything was when he had to report the assassination of President John F. Kennedy. It was my job to gather all the information I could, write the stories and prepare the voice tapes. It was Campbell's job to read the stories on-air. We were both in shock and tears much of the day. It was the most difficult task I had to perform since the Springhill Mine disaster.

The only other time I saw Campbell in any kind of distress was the day that Frank Ryan didn't leave for Bermuda. Let me explain.

Every fall, Frank and Kathleen would pack up a platoon of hackney ponies and head for their winter home in Bermuda. For some reason they always left for the airport from the station with general manager Terry Kielty behind the wheel of their Lincoln.

Departure day was undoubtedly the happiest day of the year for Campbell who had great respect and even affection for Mr. Ryan, as did most of us, but was nonetheless under great pressure from him. Campbell would watch the departure from the third-floor newsroom window, and as the Lincoln pulled away he would dance a little jig of glee. Two months of freedom!

I wasn't quite as keen about the departure because I knew that in two months time when Mr. Ryan returned I'd be in hot water. It was always the same story. Frank continued to do his "Farmer's Notebook" from Bermuda, and as this was before satellite communications, it all had to be done by long-distance telephone. You can imagine the phone bills! Half an hour a day, sometimes 45 minutes a day, long distance, Bermuda to Ottawa! Thus it was that just about the time the Ryans returned, the phone bills would pour into the station and Frank would go berserk.

As chief news editor, I was responsible for the news department budget, and as Frank's broadcast calls came through the newsroom, well, you get the picture. Down to the second floor I would be summoned. There's Frank Ryan pacing back and forth across the vast expanse of his office, telephone bills spilling from his hands. Twenty minutes of explaining that the bills are a result of his long-distance calls from Bermuda usually calms him down a bit, but for the next two months or so, it is virtually impossible to get even a pencil for the newsroom. God help anyone whose typewriter ribbon runs out!

1963 had been an especially strenuous year for Campbell Macdonald. The station wasn't doing that well, staff members seemed to leave faster than they could be hired, and CKOY was still beating our pants off. Campbell's happy little jig as the Ryans pulled away was more joyous and energetic than usual. He even broke into a little song: "They're gone, they're gone, yes indeedy, they are gone!"

He stopped in mid-chorus and I swear turned white. "Oh my God, look at this." And pointed out the window. There he was— Washington crossing the Potomac, Alexander crossing the Alps (without the elephants), Horatio at the bridge, Nelson at Trafalgar, Wellington at Waterloo, Zeus with a fistful of lightning bolts— Frank Ryan, with a mad-as-hell swing to his arms, charging up Isabella Street. No Lincoln; no Kathleen; plenty of trouble!

For awhile I feared we'd have to administer mouth-to-mouth to Campbell to get his heart started again. Fortunately, someone had a bottle of scotch stowed away for just such an emergency and Campbell finally came around.

The story gradually leaked out. Frank and Kathleen had been known in the past to disagree "slightly" upon occasion. In short, they often fought like cats and dogs. One of these "minor disagreements" sprang up in the back seat of the Lincoln during the trip to the airport. Irish tempers flared a bit. Frank avowed as to how he wasn't going anywhere with Kathleen. Kathleen replied that suited her just fine. Despite calming attempts by Terry Kielty, Frank demanded an immediate halt. So there on the Bank Street Bridge, in front of Lansdowne Park, Frank disembarked from the Lincoln, plunged into the late-November chill, and in garb intended for much warmer climes, forged his way back to the station.

Despite Campbell's worst fears, we didn't see much of Mr. Ryan for the next few days. He was obviously busy rebooking his flight because in a few days I was accepting long-distance phone calls from Bermuda again. From that point on, however, Campbell reserved his little jig until Terry returned from the airport with news that the plane had actually taken off with both travellers aboard.

There are few Canadians who have left a more lasting legacy than Frank Ryan. An entire section of Ottawa bears his name, as does a school and a park. The annual Frank Ryan Memorial Trot pays tribute to his role in building Rideau Carleton Raceway, and of course, his initials are broadcast countless times a day on the radio station he founded and which still adheres to his philosophy of community service. His sudden and shocking death in 1965 was undoubtedly a direct consequence of a blow to the head suffered during a fall he took while campaigning for mayor only a few months prior.

We can only speculate what kind of mayor he would have made, but this I can assure you: They would have been very interesting times!

• • •

Rescued

One of the most powerful and influential political figures in Canadian history is suggesting I don't have my wife trained very well. But it's not my wife who is calling, it's my brother who's got himself holed up in a Hull jail and is yelling for help.

The year is 1968, our guest speaker at the Wakefield Men's Club annual dinner is the former Premier of Quebec, the father of Quebec's so-called "Quiet Revolution," Jean Lesage. I'm going to be doing the introductions so I'm sitting next to him. Believe me, I'm more than a little intimated. This, after all, is the man who transformed Quebec into a modern, secular state from a priest-ridden backwater, ruled almost as a fiefdom by semi-dictators such as Maurice Duplessis.

The social changes came so fast and furious and the financial cost is so high that two years previous, in 1966, the voters rebelled and the guy with whom I'm trying to make idle chit-chat is now the leader of Quebec's Official Opposition but still a very powerful and highly respected man.

A very decent and personable man, too, I am learning. We find we share a passion for the Montreal Canadiens. He, like I, has just taken up golf, and as we hack away at our rubber chicken, he is about to show me a new putting grip when a waiter approaches our head table and quietly tells me there is an urgent phone call for me.

I am getting up from the table when Mr. Lesage reaches across, grasps my coat sleeve and pulls me towards him. "What's the matter, Lowell? You haven't got your wife trained better than this?"

I chuckle and say something inane.

It's not my wife on the phone, it is Paul, my half-brother from Brantford, who is spending the summer with us in Wakefield.

Paul hadn't had an easy time of it. He was only eight when his father was electrocuted while working for Brantford Hydro. He was orphaned at the age of 18 when our mother died, and he had knocked around for the past couple of years, living with friends, Phyllis (my sister, his half-sister) and my wife Kitty and me in Wakefield.

"Paul, what's the matter buddy?" He sounds more than a little scared at the other end of the line. "They've got me in jail here in Hull." His voice is rising. "For God sakes, they had a gun pointed at my head! We didn't do anything. You've got to get me out of here." Having heard all the wild stories about Quebec cops and their rubber hoses, you could tell he was on the verge of panic. I finally get the whole story out of him.

He and our next-door neighbour Mike Hammer (yes, his real name) were tooling around in Mike's new car, trying to impress goodness knows who and came whipping down the hill leading into Wakefield about 20 miles over the speed limit. They were pulled over by our local cop, a man who had acquired from some place a uniform that would have made a South American dictator proud. Enough gold braid to tie up the *Queen Mary*. You get the picture.

Speeding was bad enough, but when Mike Hammer made some smart remark about the beribboned uniform, our esteemed constable pulled his gun and pointed it directly, not at Mike's head, but at Paul's. "Holy cats!" said Paul later. "It looked like a howitzer and his hand was shaking like Elvis's hips. I thought I was a goner right then and there!

They didn't shoot him, but instead hauled him off to the Hull jail where he was now making his one and only allowed phone call.

My "rescued" half-brother Paul, years later, with Lianne's champion boxer, Lynnbarry Showtime Sierra, American and Canadian Champion.

I warn him to cool it and promise I'll rush into Hull, about 25 miles to the south, and rescue him just as soon as the speeches are over. "Don't do or say anything until I get there," I tell him.

When I resettle at the head table, Mr. Lesage gives me a raised eyebrow quizzical look. I tell him the story. He pauses for a moment. "What's your brother's name?" I tell him. "Look after my place until I get back," he says and gets up and leaves his meal. Everyone, myself included, assumes he's going to the washroom, but instead he fires off a couple of questions to one of his assistants who is hovering around, gets a phone number and dials. I am close enough to hear something of what he is saying, but my French isn't good enough to understand everything. All I know is that he is giving hell to someone and making demands in no uncertain terms.

He returns to our table with a smile but says nothing.

Less than 25 minutes later, as the father of the "Quiet Revolution" is deep into his speech, he pauses briefly at the sound of police sirens. He looks down at me and gives a subtle thumbs up, missing not a beat.

It doesn't register until something catches my attention at the doorway. There they are, Paul and Mike, broad smiles—some might say smirks—on both faces.

I don't know what Jean Lesage said to the Hull police that day, but whatever it was it certainly caught their attention. The boys were escorted back to Wakefield by not one, but two police cruisers, sirens blaring, lights flashing the entire way!

The experience obviously made a great impression on Paul. He's made a wonderful career out of police work. Today he's a staff sergeant in Brantford and even married a policewoman. He claims, though, he still can't stand the sight of gold braid.

I have to tell you another story about Paul.

It happened several years ago as I was waiting for a late-night flight to bring my present wife, Deborah, back from Vancouver. I was sitting in the Ottawa airport doing the usual thing: people watching. A flight had obviously just arrived, loaded with mostly business people.

A well-dressed man, complete with obligatory briefcase, strides purposefully past, then stops. He retraces his steps and peers down at me. Oh, oh, I think, here comes trouble! "You're Lowell Green, aren't you?" I nod yes.

He introduces himself as a vice-president of Suny Oil and tells me his story. He and a couple of his executives had been in Brantford the week previous, signing some major deal. "We were all pretty excited about it," he says, "and weren't paying the least attention about the speed we were driving. Suddenly, just at the edge of Brantford, we are pulled over and this big good-looking cop comes up. As he's examining my drivers licence, we're all trying to buffalo him, explaining about the big deal we had just signed, how it was going to be good for Brantford, but he's not buying any of it."

By now I have a good idea who the big good-looking cop is, and I'm thinking to myself, oh geez, he's going to blame me. But wait for it.

"I see you boys are from Ottawa," says the cop. All three agreed. "Do any of you happen to know of a guy named Lowell Green up there?" All three say they do. "What do you think of him?" he asks. More than a little puzzled by this line of questioning, all three claim they think he's great. "Good," says the cop, "He's my brother," and rips up the ticket!

I asked Paul later what would have happened if the guys had said they thought I was a jerk or worse. He gives me a wicked smile. "I would have nailed their hides to the wall!"

I very often come to the defence of the police, and more than a few of them in Ottawa are avid listeners. One officer in particular (I won't mention his name for obvious reasons) is a great fan and once jailed a panhandler because the guy didn't like me. Actually, there's a bit more to the story.

I had been complaining about an aggressive panhandler just outside our studios on George Street in the heart of Ottawa's major tourist area, the Market. My officer friend was listening as usual and immediately whipped down to George Street, picked this guy up and gave him a lecture.

"I didn't want to send the guy to jail," explains the cop, "so I just told him to clean up his act and stop hassling people. The next day he's back at his old stand, only this time he's got a big sign claiming police brutality. I order him into the cruiser again. I still don't want to ship this guy off to a cell, so I try to talk some sense into him."

All this time, the cop is listening to me on the radio and the panhandler interrupts his lecture to ask, "Why are you listening to that guy?" "I think he's great," says the cop. "I think he's a jerk," says the panhandler. "That's it," says the cop, "You're going to jail!" And off he goes!

· · ·

The Culvert

This may come as a big surprise to you, but not everybody likes me. This fact was emphatically driven home when I very foolishly tried to get myself elected to Parliament and people actually voted against me! A very sobering reality check, indeed.

Actually, it's all Pierre Trudeau's fault. It's 1968, Trudeaumania sweeps the country, we're all still basking in the afterglow of Expo 67, anything is possible. Or so I believe. The euphoria is such that I actually believe I can take the Liberal nomination away from the sitting member of Parliament in a nomination convention. Further evidence of my crazed state is the fact that this is the Province of Quebec, I'm an anglophone barely able to speak French, while the sitting member is a Francophone who speaks wonderful English.

There's another problem. The sitting member has a name recognition far beyond anything actually deserved. Tommy Lefebvre is a nice enough guy, but he has been little more than cannon fodder in the backbenches. If his name is mentioned once every six months in dispatches from the Commons it would be highly unusual, but in Ottawa only the Prime Minister has better name recognition.

As luck would have it (and it certainly did for Tommy), one of the largest retailers of sportswear in the Capital is an outfit called Tommy and Lefebvre. They spend buckets of money advertising their name. Furthermore, the Tommy name is one of the best known and respected in the country. Tommys have been champion skiers and football players.

I hope you get it. Tommy Lefebvre, the Liberal MP for the Pontiac—Tommy and Lefebvre, the retailer spending thousands to publicize their name. Given the fact that about one third of the Canadian population has difficulty following the storyline of the "Simpsons," you can see how confusion might arise!

If that's not enough, Tommy Lefebvre has a secret weapon. Secret, until my campaign team learns of it the night before the nomination convention in Maniwaki.

Throughout the campaign, it has been a battle between the voters of the old riding of the Pontiac, encompassing places like Shawville, Quyon and Campbell's Bay. My supporters are mostly in the former Gatineau Riding, including Wakefield, Low, Farrelton and Maniwaki. The two ridings have merged for the 1968 election.

The secret weapon is the Hilton Mine, the largest employer in the Pontiac. Somehow Tommy Lefebvre's people have convinced the mine manager to shut the entire place down for nomination day, load all 200 or so employees into buses and ferry them to the voting at the Maniwaki arena. To ensure that the "right guy" wins, the luggage compartments of the buses have been loaded down with some of Molson's finest. The word is if the "right guy" wins, the luggage compartments get opened on the trip home. This is, after all, Quebec!

Here's where I make my big mistake.

There is only one road leading from the Pontiac to Maniwaki. It slices through the mountain separating the Pontiac from the Gatineau and runs directly through the small town of Otter Lake. Running beneath the road, just east of Otter Lake, is a large culvert.

The McLaughlin brothers, Peter and Dwight, who have been handling my campaign, have a plan. "We're going to rip that culvert out of there tonight," they inform me. "Joey Peck has the front-end loader all ready. It shouldn't take any more than a couple of hours and it will stop those buses cold!"

Not that familiar with Quebec politics, I am naturally aghast. "We can't do that," I say. The McLaughlins and several others in attendance are shocked. They can't understand my reluctance. They are emphatic. "Let those buses and the beer through and you're a dead duck!" In the end the candidate, that's me, wins the debate. (And loses the nomination.)

The next day, right on schedule, several big buses, looking mightily weighted down, pull into the parking lot of the Maniwaki arena and my goose (or duck) is cooked.

We put up a good fight. I give a great speech in both English and French. We have a big band there. It's the biggest thing to hit Maniwaki in years, but I know I'm losing when a guy comes staggering up and points a finger in my face.

It's pretty obvious the buses have already opened their luggage compartments. Either that or this guy has a personal supply stashed away. The fact he can barely stand has apparently not hindered his ability to vote.

"I voted against you," he manages to say. Then waving his finger back and forth for emphasis he adds, "Four times!"

When it's all over, we find that 822 registered delegates have cast 1,192 votes!

Do I protest? Are you kidding? This is Quebec!

That culvert, by the way, is still there. Darn.

• • •

October Terror

Charlotte Gobeil was a beautiful, talented CBC-TV broadcaster perhaps best known for having dated Prime Minister Pierre Elliot Trudeau. She was, from all reports, a staunch federalist during the FLQ crisis in Quebec. Her brother, Jean Gobeil, was a next-door neighbour of ours near Wakefield, Quebec. He was a kind and gentle man but an avowed separatist who may have saved our children's lives. Here is what happened:

On October 5, 1970, British Trade Minister James Cross is kidnapped from his home in Montreal by members of the Liberation cell of the Front de Libération du Québec (FLQ). The FLQ releases a list of demands for Cross's safe release, which include:

- The release of 23 "political prisoners";
- $500,000 in gold;
- the broadcast and publication of the FLQ manifesto;
- the publication of the names of the police informants for terrorist activities;
- an aircraft to take the kidnappers to Cuba or Algeria;
- the rehiring of the Lapalme postal truck drivers;
- the cessation of all police search activities.

October 6—Prime Minister Pierre Trudeau announces that any decision regarding the FLQ will be taken jointly by the Federal and Quebec governments. Several newspapers publish the FLQ manifesto or parts of it.

October 7—about 30 people are arrested in police raids.

October 10—Quebec's Minister of Labour, Pierre Laporte, is kidnapped from his home in St. Lambert, a South Shore suburb of Montreal. The Chenier cell of the FLQ claims credit.

October 11—Laporte pleads for his life in a letter sent to Quebec Premier Robert Bourassa. The Quebec Cabinet negotiates with the FLQ but the talks break down after two days.

October 12—Prime Minister Trudeau sends troops to guard the homes of MPs and diplomats in Ottawa. Tanks patrol the streets!

October 13—CBC reporter Tim Ralfe asks Trudeau how far he is prepared to go to stop the FLQ. Trudeau responds, "Just watch me!"

October 15—Premier Robert Bourassa asks for help from the Canadian Armed Forces. Some 7,500 troops are deployed in Ottawa, Montreal and Quebec City.

During a Cabinet meeting that runs into the early hours of the morning, Prime Minister Trudeau announces he is imposing the War Measures Act, the first and only time it has ever been enacted in peace time. Within 48 hours, 250 people are arrested.

October 17—My wife Kitty and I are having breakfast in the dining room of the Caswell Motor Hotel in Sudbury. The room falls silent as the radio is turned up. The body of Pierre Laporte has just been found in the trunk of a car in the St. Hubert Airport parking lot near Montreal. He has been strangled with the chain of the crucifix hanging around his neck. There is a collective gasp of horror in the dining room and across the nation.

Kitty and I have been very reluctant to leave our Wakefield area home in light of the fear stalking Quebec for the past month, but with relative quiet for the past 10 days, we decide to attend the funeral of a close friend in Sudbury. We leave our two young daughters at home in the care of their grandmother. The news of the Laporte murder sends us scrambling with fear back to our room. We are throwing clothes into our suitcase, preparing for the long dash home when the phone rings. It is Jean Gobiel, our next-door neighbour and leading separatist. I will never forget the words:

"Lowell, Jean Gobiel here. Listen you had better get your children out of that house. There are some crazy people saying some crazy things!" I can hardly catch my breath. "What crazy people? Where are they? What do you mean?" My heart is pounding; my hands shake. Kitty's face is chalk white. "Crazy people is all," says Jean, "I have to go."

We immediately phone home. Kitty's mother answers on the first ring. "Ella," I say with as much calm as I can muster, "get the girls out of the house right now. Get them into your car and drive them to your place in Ottawa. Don't worry about clothes or anything. Get them out of there right now. We'll be home as soon as we can."

Ella suspected something was up when Jean had phoned her just a few minutes before to get our phone number in Sudbury, and she already has Lianne and Danielle dressed and ready to go. All she says is, "Don't worry, they'll be safe."

She was right. God bless her!

Were they ever in real danger? Who can say? I questioned Jean many times about his strange phone call, but he refused to elaborate. Did someone tip him off that our children were in danger? Was he at a meeting someplace where their names cropped up? To this day I am not sure.

Prior to October 17, Jean and I had developed a fairly close relationship. After that date, he became distant and dropped out of our lives; shortly after, I believe, he moved away.

It was one of the most frightening episodes of our lives. Danielle, who was nine when it all happened, and Lianne, who was seven, had no idea of the drama unfolding around them and today have only vague memories of the entire FLQ crisis.

My novel *Death in October* was inspired by the events of those truly frightening days.

On December 3, James Cross is released when the FLQ members holding him negotiate passage to Cuba. Paul Rose and Francis Simard receive life sentences for the murder. Bernard Lortie is sentenced to 20 years for kidnapping. In December 1982, Paul Rose is granted a full parole. The five FLQ members who fled to Cuba are later found to be living in Paris, France. Over the years all five return to Canada to face trial. They are all convicted of kidnapping and sentenced to jail terms ranging from 20 months to two years. All are free today.

. . .

The Joke

As a player and coach with the Ottawa Rough Riders during their glory years, there was no fiercer competitor than George Brancato, the last man to coach a Grey Cup winning team in the Capital (1976). He was exactly the same in the handball court. George would sooner die (or kill you) than lose. I've seen him run full tilt into a wall in an attempt to retrieve the ball. How he hasn't shattered every bone in his body by now is a miracle.

The thing he hated almost as much as losing was being interrupted during a heated game. As coach of the Rough Riders, the demands on him were terrific and as far as he was concerned his time in the court was sacred. His instructions to the staff at the downtown YMCA were that he was not to be disturbed during a handball game unless it was the general manager Frank Clair or the media. "I don't want some nutcase reporter upsetting my players with some crazy story about a trade or something," he explained. And as for Frank Clair, well you just didn't ignore Frank Clair.

Every once in a while some reporter would call with some question or other and a very reluctant "Y" employee would drag himself down to the handball courts, knock very timidly on the door and announce that so and so of such and such a paper or station wanted to speak with Mr. Brancato. The reaction was totally predictable and volatile. First there would be dead silence in the court, including from Brancato's opponent who knew only too well what was on the way. It was especially dangerous if George happened to be losing. The swearing would start softly, rising in volume to a truly monumental peak as he kicked the door to the court open and stomped into the dressing room, viciously yanked the phone off the hook and yelled, "Ya." It was, all in all, a great performance, much appreciated by all of us witnesses who tried desperately to stifle laughs.

My buddy and handball partner Paul (Punchy) Lapointe and I were soaking up a Fresca one afternoon, having just wrapped up a rousing game of handball, when Punchy remarked that we hadn't been treated recently to one of George's performances. We were sitting just outside the courts and could hear George and some poor victim going at it hammer and tong. You knew it was Brancato by the sound of flesh thudding into walls.

We looked at each other and somewhere a light bulb went off!

We had a rookie sports announcer at CFRA, so I figured he would be perfect. In as conspiratorial a voice as I could muster, I tell the by now highly excited rookie that I have just learned that the Rough Riders have signed Y.A. Title, the NFL Hall of Fame New York Giant quarterback, to a long-term contract with the Rough Riders. "Look," I tell the rookie, "the guy who can confirm this for you is Coach George Brancato, and I happen to know he's at the downtown "Y" right now. Call the "Y" and insist on talking to George and he'll give you the scoop of a lifetime."

Actually the story wasn't as crazy as it sounded since Title had retired from the Giants the year previously after setting just about every passing record in the books.

Punchy and I then sit there, eagerly awaiting the phone call and the "performance." And we wait and wait. Nothing. No call. George finally emerges from the court, wiping sweat and a big grin from his face, having just chalked up another victory.

I just shrug my shoulders. "Guess the rookie wasn't so stupid after all," I say. "Ah well, maybe next time!"

We decide to plan another attack over a steak at Al's just up the road a bit. En route, we turn the car radio on to our signature sports show of the day, "Sports at Six." First item. A breathless rookie with this: *CFRA Sports has learned on good authority that the Ottawa Rough Riders have signed NFL all-star quarterback Y.A. Title to a long-term contract. Title was introduced into the Football Hall of Fame in 1971 and has established numerous passing records in his long and distinguished career with the New York Giants.*

I look at Punchy. He is as white as a sheet. He looks at me and tells me I look like a guy who had just lost his job and his testicles. I don't know about the body parts, but I am pretty sure my job is history. What the heck happened anyway?

Well, here's what happened. The rookie, who by the way has long since disappeared into the archives of failed sportscasters, had become so excited about the Y.A. Title part that he didn't hear me suggesting that George Brancato confirm the story.

This guy decides to go right to the top. General Manager Frank Clair himself.

Frank isn't in his office, his staff tells him, but can probably be paged as he waits for a flight at Pearson Airport in Toronto. Lo and behold, Frank Clair is paged repeatedly throughout Pearson International Airport! Fortunately, Frank either doesn't hear or doesn't recognize his name and doesn't respond to the page. The rookie, deciding that I was a pretty reliable source, decides to run the story without confirmation. The rest, as they say, is history.

It caused a considerable stir in the community, let me tell you. We even got calls from New York media outlets, *Sports Illustrated*, and so on. It was all pretty difficult to explain.

Fortunately, our sports director Ernie Calcutt, who among other skills was one of the best football play-by-play announcers in the country, had a wonderful sense of humour. Instead of chewing me out, hauling me on the carpet or whatever other punishment was allowed in the '70s, Ernie laughed himself crazy and told the whole story to his listeners the next morning.

I will not reveal what George Brancato said to Punchy and me the next day at the "Y." Suffice to say that for about the next year or so, I had to respond to the name: Y. eh!

· · ·

Charlotte's Boy Toy

There are some today who believe that Charlotte Whitton was a lesbian. At the very least, she appeared to have no interest in men, certainly not in later life. I have some news for you: I think she was interested in me. Don't laugh. I've been around long enough to know when a woman is interested.

The year is 1960. I'm 24. Charlotte is 64. I'm single, new in town with a bit of a Montreal swagger still to my stride. It's municipal election night. Charlotte Whitton is winning the mayoralty and I'm doing live broadcasts from her Centretown headquarters. I catch her looking at me a of couple times. Nothing blatant, nothing overtly flirtatious, but there's a hint of a glint there I have seen before. At the time, I thought it was because I represented the radio station owned by her brother-in-law. But as I later learned, there was no love lost there, so you tell me what she was up to!

About halfway through the night, Charlotte suddenly announces that anyone who wishes to interview her, or even talk to her, must first check with me. This astounds and embarrasses me since I'm new on the municipal beat. Some of the reporters in the room have been covering City Hall for years. Much to my chagrin this goes on all night. Veteran reporters first must come to me and ask for an interview with Charlotte Whitton.

With Charlotte winning handily, there is a noisy motorcade up Metcalfe Street to City Hall for a reception and party. At Charlotte's insistence, I find myself in her limousine leading the parade. Our chauffeur, Charlotte Whitton and a more than slightly puzzled Lowell Green. I remember it well since one of Ottawa's finest stopped us to remind the Mayor of the anti-noise bylaw, which she had passed in a previous administration. She is in great spirits and thinks this is hilarious.

Charlotte was, of course, swamped with congratulations and well wishes at the party. I snuck away as soon as I could, but for the better part of a year as I covered City Hall, there is no question I was given preferential treatment, which often caused resentment amongst other reporters. Nothing ever happened, of course. Charlotte Whitton was many things, but beautiful she was definitely not.

I have no way of knowing if it was anything other than a desire to bug the City Hall reporting establishment. But I'll tell you this. If I were placing bets with a couple of "Valley lads," I'd give them at least even odds that Charlotte Whitton, even at age 64, wasn't quite as disinterested in men as most believe!

• • •

The Coach

There are a million stories about Frank Clair, undoubtedly the finest coach and general manager in the history of the CFL. He's the man, of course, after whom Frank Clair Stadium is named, where the Ottawa Renegades now play. I won't repeat all the stories about him (you can read them elsewhere), but there is one story that is as typical of Frank as any.

I was attending a party at the home of Don Holtby, who a little later became general manager of the Rough Riders himself. Frank Clair ambles up and we start the usual cocktail party chit-chat. I have always hated idle talk, so I think I'll take the opportunity to get to know a bit more about this man who plays such an important role in the community. I had heard that aside from his passion for football, Frank Clair had few other interests. Football and that's pretty well it, was the word around town.

"Frank," I say, "what do you do with yourself when you aren't involved with football?" He looks kind of blankly at me. "Do you have any hobbies? What do you do in your spare time?" At this Frank brightens. "I love to fish." This peaks my interest since I have been spending a good deal of time trying to hook onto "the big one" in the St. Lawrence. "Oh really? What do you fish for?" Once again a kind of blank look.

I change the subject a bit. "Where do you fish?" He is quick to reply. "Ah…up there in Quebec." I wait. "I forget the name of the lake," he says. This hardly surprises me since Frank has been known to forget the name of his star quarterback Russ Jackson, usually referring to him as number 12. "Do you get up there much?" I ask. "Oh ya," he says. "I love fishing." I ask the natural question. "When was the last time you were up there?" Frank stares off into space for a moment or two. "Weeellll...I was up there last year, wasn't I? No...I guess it was two years ago."

I did what any person with half a brain would do: dropped fishing and hobbies and started talking football!

· · ·

Gzowski

Somewhere in the bowels of that monster of a CBC building in Toronto is a video which Peter Gzowski always claimed was the funniest thing he ever saw. For years, when things really got rolling during "Mother Corp" Christmas parties, someone would say "Hey, where's that hee-haw video?" They'd haul it out of the archives, plug it onto the big screen in the lobby, and once again the place would explode in laughter. For all I know, even though Peter Gzowski is no longer with us, the video is still bringing the house down.

Most Canadians remember Peter Gzowski with great fondness. For years he dominated morning radio in Canada. His "Morningside" program was one of the finest things CBC radio ever did. Peter's deliberately hesitant, sometimes almost stuttering, style seemed to fit the country perfectly during more innocent times. With Gzowski, even recipes were fascinating and somehow seemed...well...so Canadian!

Towards the end of his career, his appeal began to wane, probably because of demands for political correctness from a series of incredibly incompetent CBC executives, but for the better part of 15 years, Gzowski helped to define a Canadian identity. Not a flag-waving kind of patriotism but a subtle sense of community with a common thread of shared experience.

As with most highly successful people, Gzowski had experienced more than a little failure and disappointment. He left his successful CBC radio show "This Country in the Morning" in the early 1970s to try his hand at television. The resultant show, "90 Minutes Live," was terrible. Fortunately, he returned to radio in the early '80s with "Morningside" and became a Canadian icon. Despite his apparent ease on radio, Gzowski was an uncomfortable television performer. For the most part, he hated what he was doing on television and it showed.

One of the few shows which Gzowski always maintained he enjoyed thoroughly was shot at my father's farm near Ormstown in Quebec's Eastern Townships.

My father called it a farm but it was more accurately a menagerie with every conceivable kind of animal running helter-skelter loose. Belted Galloway cattle, Landrace hogs, sheep of every description and colour, including a ram that would attack on sight anything red. Bulldogs, boxers and springer spaniels were under-foot everywhere. For a time he had a monkey and a buffalo. At any given time, there would be at least 25 different breeds of exotic chickens, many of them roaming everywhere, including on the front porch of his old stone farmhouse. And his favourite—a large, very stubborn and, I suspect, very smart donkey.

The film crew arrived early one morning and set up shop. Gzowski was obviously fascinated with the farm, which included a second stone house jammed with artifacts and memorabilia. He later told friends that he found my father to be one of the most intelligent and interesting men he had ever met. The feature shot that day has been shown a number of times on "Life and Times" and you can clearly see the rapport between the two men. Gzowski looks relaxed and is obviously enjoying himself.

What you didn't see on CBC's "90 Minutes Live" when it was

originally screened, nor do you see now on "Life and Times," is that hilarious clip that so entertains CBC staff.

The "shoot" has gone well during the day, but the time is getting late and the light beginning to fade as they prepare the final scene. This is to show my father, wearing his beaten-up old felt hat (which Dennis the donkey had partially consumed), stepping out of his front door onto the dog-filled porch, lighting up his pipe and making a little speech about the joys of country living. The first time the cameras roll, my father drops his pipe.

Take two: This time all the dogs suddenly take off after a squirrel and several precious minutes of light are lost while they get a couple of the dogs off the chase and back onto the porch.

My father, at the best of times, could not be described as a patient man. By the time the dogs settle down, he is getting what could be described as "testy."

Take three: He fumbles his lines.

A member of the lighting crew now makes a big mistake when he says, "Mr. Green, we're losing the light. This will have to be our final take."

At this, my father starts to get red under the collar and mumbles a few choice words.

Take four: It goes perfectly. The "star" steps out of his door, looks skyward, takes his pipe, lights it. Reaches down and pats an appreciative springer on the head. The springer licks his hand as the camera zooms in. Perfect! My father finds a block of wood, sets his foot upon it, takes the pipe out of his mouth and sweeps it around to demonstrate the magnificence of his surroundings.

Leaning directly into the camera, he opens his mouth to begin the soliloquy about country life he has spent days crafting and practising. Out of his mouth comes the most ungodly sound God ever gave to one of his creatures: Hee haw! hee haw! hee haw! hee haw! Actually it's more eeeeeeh aaaaaaw! Eeeeeeh aaaaaaw! Awful! Terrible!

It's feeding time for Dennis the donkey.

The shocked crew continues to roll film as my father rips off his old felt hat, throws it to the porch floor, takes his pipe and throws it on top of the offending hat, then swearing a blue streak, jumps with both feet onto the pile he has thus created. The dogs scatter and run for cover!

It is one of filmdom's great moments and I have always suspected that had CBC had the courage and good sense to run that scene, "90 Minutes Live" would have gone down in history as one of the CBC's greatest successes!

• • •

The General

I pull my car into the CFRA parking lot on Isabella Street and here is this funny-looking little fat guy decked out in some kind of Civil War uniform, complete with long sweeping sword, inspecting a regiment of Canadian soldiers. What the h…is this?

The funny little fat guy with the big sword is, of course, Ken "the General" Grant. I forget which regiment he was inspecting, but I suspect their commanding officer got called up on the carpet once news of this little escapade leaked out. And there was no chance news wouldn't leak out, since the whole thing was being broadcast live on one of only two private radio stations in the Nation's Capital.

The stunt was typical of the brilliance of Ken's ability to promote himself, his show and CFRA. Despite a horrendous childhood, Ken had, through sheer determination and hard work, created one of the most successful broadcast personas in Canada.

Ernie Calcutt, Lowell Green, General Grant and CFRA general manager Terry Kielty. Must be a bow-tie convention!

Calcutt, Green and Grant who dominated the basepaths with the Happy Blunderers and the airwaves for more than a decade. Did a funny little hamster change the course of broadcast history in the Capital?

A whole generation of Ottawans were marched off to school by Ken "the General" Grant who from the early 1960s to the mid 1990s ran the most successful local morning radio show in Canada. His ratings consistently outranked those of all others. For all I know, it may have been the most successful morning show on private radio in North America.

There was nothing Ken wouldn't do to get a laugh or build an audience. For years he was available to speak to any group of any size, anywhere, anytime, and was a terrific entertainer. One of his favourite acts was to slip away while various guest speakers were addressing major events, then reappear at the end of each speech with a different and flamboyant change of clothing. By the third such switch in plumage, the crowd always caught on and gave him a big hand. Inevitably it culminated in a standing ovation when he appeared after the final speech in his Civil War uniform. Classic General Grant.

Ken, especially in his early years at CFRA, was a man driven to succeed and wasn't easy to get to know. We travelled a good deal together around the Ottawa and St. Lawrence Valleys playing softball with the CFRA Happy Blunderers, but I can't say I ever felt close to him until the incident in the "crow's nest."

Today there are some 18 radio stations serving the Ottawa-Gatineau market, but in the 1960s there were only two private stations: CFRA and CKOY. CKOY had been the big winner in the ratings war until the powerful troika of Ernie Calcutt, General Grant and Lowell Green came along. By the mid '60s, CFRA was whomping the competition, including a couple of new stations that had arrived on the scene. Whomping the competition in radio means you have the lion's share of the audience and are making a ton of money. Today, for example, just one half-percentage point of audience share can mean as much as half a million dollars in revenue. CKOY tried everything to scuttle us; they imported some big-name stars, but nothing they did could make a dint in the size of our audience. The money rolled in!

In desperation, CKOY sent a message to me: If Ernie Calcutt, General Grant and Lowell Green will defect to CKOY, we will pay the three of you whatever you want. Just name your price. A blank cheque awaits!

Wow!!

Ernie Calcutt, who has management aspirations, immediately turns it down, but both Ken and I have young families and we have to look at this very closely. Ken has just built a beautiful and innovative home in the Gatineau hills of Quebec and calls a meeting to be held there the following day.

A moving van is unloading household items and furniture as I pull into his driveway. Ken's new girlfriend, Gale, the woman he would later marry, has just decided to move in with him. Things are a bit chaotic in the living room, so Ken suggests we retire to the "crow's nest."

This is a neat little office Ken has built on top of his house. The only way to reach it is up a ladder through a hole in the "crow's nest" floor. The view up there is spectacular.

Ken and I are deep in discussion about the offer. One of our main dilemmas is just exactly what does a blank cheque mean. CKOY had said we could name our own price, but obviously there has to be a limit. What is the best way to determine that limit? And, of course, we are both very happy at CFRA. Do we really want to leave for any price?

I suggest we each determine how much money it would take to move us from CFRA, write this down on a piece of paper, along with any other terms, and then when we have finished we will show each other our figure and terms and go with the richest.

We are both busily scratching out a few proposals when suddenly a pretty but very tear-stained face pokes up through the hole in the floor. "Barney's dead," she sobs. It is Gale, clutching the ladder with both hands and thus unable to wipe away the tears that by now cascade down her face.

"Oh God, no," groans Ken, who immediately drops everything and, with soothing words, follows her down the ladder. I am totally in the dark. Has there been a tragic accident? Who is Barney? Should I do something? Say something? Give my condolences? All thoughts of money and changing stations are vanquished.

After about half an hour, I am about to head down that ladder myself when Ken suddenly reappears looking very sad indeed. I mumble something about condolences and should I leave and who is Barney. It is all I can do to stifle laughter when Ken very gravely informs me that Barney is Gale's pet hamster, who apparently was not at all pleased with the move from Gale's house and has registered a very powerful objection by simply flipping "paws up" in his cage.

I can see Ken is really upset about the whole thing, so I suggest we postpone our meeting to a later date when suddenly up through the hole in the floor what should appear but a face beaming from ear to ear. "Barney's alive, Ken! Barney's alive! Come and see!" Gale's face disappears with Ken following in hot pursuit. I just shake my head in wonderment. What the h…!

It's true, Barney is alive. He had never been dead. I once owned a pet shop so I should have known. Hamsters, when frightened, will sometimes "play possum," that is pretend to play dead. His "paws up" performance was apparently prompted by Ken's little Boston terrier sniffing around the cage.

When I leave them, Ken and Gale are in each other's arms softly crying with joy.

We never again discussed that offer from CKOY.

The history of broadcasting in the National Capital might have been very different if a funny little hamster hadn't decided to play games!

The only time Ken really got mad at me was when I hit him square in the butt with a softball while a few hundred people roared with laughter.

The Happy Blunderers were playing in Morrisburg, a lovely little Seaway town about an hour's drive south of Ottawa. Most of our players worked for CFRA, but very often we inserted a few ringers, depending upon the skill of the team we would be playing against. It was always more fun to have a competitive game, besides which, even though these were all fun games to raise charitable dollars, Ken hated to lose. One of these ringers was a very friendly guy I'll call Vic who had a couple of teenaged sons who often liked to accompany their father to games around the Valley.

Vic offered to drive me to the Morrisburg game. "It'll be fun," Vic assures me. Since Vic has a large repertoire of off-colour jokes, I presume that's what he's talking about. Big mistake.

We have barely cleared the city limits when the unmistakable aroma of marijuana begins to float up from the back seat where his two sons are giggling away. This is the '60s, please remember!

It isn't long until one of the joints is being passed around, and here I admit it, I took a couple of puffs. By the time we arrive, both Vic and I think Morrisburg is the funniest place we've ever seen. The ball field is even funnier. The large crowd we determine to be hilarious. I am pitching. Vic is playing first base. By the time the first inning is over, Ken is fuming. He knows something is up, but isn't sure what.

"Have you guys been drinking?" he growls. We both shake our heads in absolute truth and complete innocence. "Whatever you two are doing, stop it," orders Ken. "We're here to play ball not play the fool." We try to explain it's all in fun, but "the General" isn't buying it.

The second inning is worse. I am throwing the ball up in the air, rolling it along the ground, all the time laughing. The crowd loves it. They think it's all part of the act. At each antic, including a silly little dance by Vic, the crowd roars even more. After about the third ball I've rolled along the ground, Ken comes storming out from behind the plate where he has been catching. He unleashes a few choice words in my general direction and threatens to kick me out of the game if I don't stop fooling around.

He stomps back, mumbling something under his breath and bends over to pick up his catcher's mask behind the plate. Terrible judgement. The temptation is far too great. I let loose with perhaps one of the most accurate pitches ever thrown by any ball player at any time in history. Dead centre in the middle of the wonderful big target staring me in the face as he bends over. It almost knocks him bum over teakettle. As close to perfect as you can get.

The crowd goes wild! So does "the General"!

Vic and I spend the rest of the game watching the big ships in the St. Lawrence Seaway or something like that. Everyone tells me the game wasn't nearly as much fun after we left. Vic insists to this day we got a "bum" deal.

• • •

The Greenline

Talk radio is launched in Ottawa with the host being hanged in effigy by the charwomen of Parliament Hill. It's November 1960; Joe Pyne is advising Montreal callers to "go gargle with razor blades" and whomping all competitors with his ratings.

Ottawa's CKOY decides to give it a try. Bill Kincaid, fresh in from the far north, is doing just about everything else at the station, so why not run him up the flagpole and see if he flies.

"Geeze," says Bill today, "women were so mad they almost blew up the station. I went on the air that first day suggesting that if housewives were really organized they could easily have all their housework done in an hour and ten minutes!" He laughs. "Not only did the cleaning women on Parliament Hill hang me in effigy, things got so heated at the National Press Club I couldn't go near the place for weeks!" If you know Bill, you understand what a serious blow that was!

"Live Wire," as that first historic show is called, is a sensation. Ottawa has never heard anything like it. Talk radio is in its infancy. Aside from Joe Pyne in Montreal, there are fewer than a dozen such shows in all of North America in 1960. CKOY leaps ahead in the ratings when "Live Wire" is on the air, and until 1966 leaves CFRA and all comers in the dust.

Despite his huge success, Bill Kincaid lasts only until May of 1962 when he and station manager Johnny Murphy have a falling out. Murphy, according to Kincaid, insisted that all topics be approved by him before being aired, something Kincaid wanted no part of.

Now comes a bit of history even I wasn't aware of until recently. A man named Peter Griffin replaced Bill Kincaid as host of "Live Wire." Don't think your mind is abandoning you if you don't remember him. He went down in flames after only about six weeks when he let some goofball ramble on about Shoppers City (one of the first shopping centres in Ottawa) being a "rook joint." As you might imagine, Shoppers City and Loeb took serious offence at this and immediately pulled their advertising from CKOY—a huge loss of revenue.

Scary guy, right? This was part of an advertising campaign for "The Greenline."

This hitherto ignored bit of trivia had a profound affect on the history of broadcasting in Ottawa and, just incidentally, my life.

Shortly after Bill Kincaid left CKOY, Frank Ryan approached him and persuaded him to launch a talk show on CFRA. At the time, I had no idea this was in the wind. Frank brought Bill around and introduced him to me in the newsroom at 150 Isabella. I was chief news editor at the time. I don't recall that day, but Bill tells me I made a huge impression on him since I was pounding a reluctant typewriter with my fist and scarcely mumbled a greeting.

In the midst of the negotiations with Bill, the "rook joint" fallout hit the fan and CFRA panicked. At the time, Loeb was a major sponsor on CFRA with Jim Marino (there's a name from the past) conducting his "IGA—I Give Away" contest just about every hour of the day. "Good God," said a white-faced sales manager, George Gowling, "talk shows are too damn dangerous." And so the idea died right there. Bill Kincaid worked at CFRA for about a year hosting various programs, but never did a radio talk show again.

A rambling idiot on the Peter Griffin show thus determined my career in talk radio! There is no doubt that if Bill Kincaid, an

If you can find a sillier picture, please let me know. My wife will kill me when she sees this published. That's Hal Anthony on the left and, yes, me holding the pail. The referee is Miss Ottawa Rough Rider for that year, Marlene Shepherd. Hal was still working for CKOY and thus enemy #1. We somehow were persuaded to enter a milking contest at the Central Canada Exhibition, a contest I won easily. Hal, a prairie boy, knew nothing about milking cows. I grew up squirting milk at barn cats and knew all the tricks. Right after this picture was taken, Hal began chatting up a fan while I stroked old bossy's udder, prepping her for the big contest. I got half a pail in the allotted three minutes; Hal got barely a squirt and claimed I had tricked him, which I had. We later became fast friends.

extremely talented broadcaster, had launched a talk show on CFRA, "The Greenline" would never have been born, certainly not in Ottawa.

Now move the calendar ahead about four years. Mac Lipson's career as host of "Live Wire" is brought to a sudden and sad halt by the murder of a young woman in Ottawa, whose body is found wrapped in a dry-cleaning bag. Mac at one time knew the woman; he's questioned by police, who determine he played no role. However, rumours persist, fueled by an incredibly cruel statement from Mayor Charlotte Whitton. Mac is interviewing the mayor, pressing her for some answers concerning some municipal affair when Charlotte, in a fit of temper, turns on him and says something to the effect that she should be careful what she says if she doesn't want to end up smothered in a dry-cleaning bag. Most of us who knew Mac agree he was never the same again.

Unable to continue, Mac's hosting duties on "Live Wire" are now taken over by CKOY news director Hal Anthony, a man everyone at CFRA thoroughly detests. Hal Anthony, in fact, is enemy number one with us on Isabella Street primarily because of his prowess as a curler. Each year, the CKOY curling team, skipped by Hal Anthony, soundly beats the CFRA team, skipped usually by Ken "The General" Grant. Hal, it must be explained, was not a graceful winner. Much boasting and derision concerning both our curling and broadcasting abilities was his style.

So when I got a call in May 1966 from Hal Anthony asking me if I was interested in taking over as host of "Live Wire," I was more than a little astonished. I was stirring things up pretty good at CFRA with investigative reporting and commentaries, but I had to admit the idea of hosting a talk show was intriguing. So was the money: CKOY was offering $15,000 a year, about $5,000 more than I was making at CFRA.

The next morning I was in CFRA general manager Terry Kielty's office to report my conversation. Terry's response is still vivid in my mind. He leaned back in his chair, stroked his nose between thumb and forefinger a few times and said, "Hmm, hmm, maybe we should try one of those."

And so we did. We still didn't have a name for the show, when on a flight back from Toronto, I met Bill Casey, an old friend then working for the CBC. Bill was excited for me. "You've got to call it 'The Greenline,'" he said. And so we did. We launched in June of 1966; the show immediately shot to number one in the ratings and remained there until the day we retired it, July 1, 1978. It was the longest running, most successful radio talk show in Canadian history. That is until the Lowell Green Show came along!

• • •

Diet

Over the years, I have become a certified expert of tongue-lashings. From callers to bosses to girlfriends, wives, even bums on the street, I have been "straightened out" so frequently and so eloquently there is none in the land more expert on judging the quality of catching hell than I.

Thus I can say with great certainty that never in my life have I experienced a more competent tongue-lashing than one unleashed on me by John George Diefenbaker, Leader of Her Majesty's Opposition, former Prime Minister of Canada.

Like so many great mistakes that dog our lives, mine started out innocently enough with the best of intentions. My talk show that particular day was on the changing social climate of the 1960s. We talked a bit about how just a few years ago Roman Catholic parents refused to allow their daughters to marry Protestants and how regressive that now seemed. Then we got into the changing attitudes towards divorce. "It used to be," I said, "that a divorced man or woman had little or no chance of success as a politician. The stigma was just too great."

Here I stepped into quicksand. "On the other hand," I said, "look at John and Olive Diefenbaker. The fact that Olive is a divorced woman in no way impeded Mr. Diefenbaker's career; in fact, it is a matter of no consequence to the voters." Or words to that effect.

I was in the Thelen Torontow Lighting Centre on Bank Street in downtown Ottawa when the station tracked me down and the "boom" was lowered. Our program director sounded frightened on the phone. Small wonder. He'd just been shaken by a 15-minute Diefenbaker "warm up" barrage. "What the hell did you say?" he gasps. "You'd better get back here to the station as fast as you can and call the old guy before he comes down here and blows the place up!"

Memory is a funny thing. You cannot recall pain with any clarity, which is why most of what our former Prime Minister had to say to me that afternoon has slipped my mind. One phrase, however, rings as clear as a bell, probably because I have heard versions of it several times at the Shakespearean Festival in Stratford.

Dief's soliloquy went something like this: "Ahh, I have experienced the slings and arrows of merciless, vicious attacks all my life. I have come to expect that. Ahh, but this is as low as it has ever gone. When they attack me, I say stand fast, be brave. Ahh, but when they attack my wife, well, that goes too far. Too far, I say! Too far! Never in my experience has my wife had to endure the slings and arrows of this kind of unwarranted, outrageous attack. You say, Mr. Green, that my wife was divorced. That is a clear and blatant lie. My wife was widowed. Ahh, this goes too far. Too far! Too far!"

All this time I'm trying to get a word in edgewise, apologizing, trying to explain that if a mistake was made here it was without intent to harm in any way. I doubt he heard a word of it. As he finally hangs up he is still mumbling about too far—too far.

It was all my father's fault. He had gone to school in Arthur with Olive and swore until the day he died that she had divorced her first husband and that the story about her being a widow was not true. When I mentioned this on the air, I just assumed it was common knowledge she was divorced. Obviously, either my father was wrong or John didn't have a clear picture.

My falling-out with Dief didn't affect the relationship I had with his brother Elmer.

It is now generally known that Elmer was, as we used to say in those days, "a little slow." But he loved animals and especially tropical fish, so almost every day Olive would pack him off to visit our pet shop on Sparks Street in downtown Ottawa. Actually, I'm not sure if Olive pointed him in our direction or if his wanderings just naturally drew him to us. We didn't mind at all. Elmer was a real gentleman—quiet, polite and never in the way. He was very gentle with all animals, so upon occasion my wife would ask him to catch a hamster or guinea pig for a customer. Elmer's eyes would light up at this and he would accomplish the task with aplomb.

Sometimes, as the hour grew late, he would leave of his own accord and make his way back the few blocks to Sussex Drive and Stornoway where he was living with John and Olive. Occasionally, however, the phone would ring and Olive would very politely ask, "Is Elmer there?" If our answer was yes, she would say, "Could you please send him home?" He stopped coming one day for no apparent reason and we missed him.

My good friend the late Hal Anthony, told one of the best John Diefenbaker stories. Hal was reading morning news on CFRA when

Diefenbaker wrote his first book. As a great fan of "the Chief," Hal hauled himself down to a local bookstore one morning, stood in line for half an hour or so and got the author to personally sign the book.

"To whom would you like me to address this?" asked Diefenbaker.

"If you don't mind, Mr. Diefenbaker, could you make it out to me, Hal Anthony."

At this, Dief's eyes shot up from the table. "Hal Anthony! Hal Anthony! I listen to you every morning. Ahh, you are wonderful; wonderful. You come from my riding, don't you?"

"Yes, I do," replied Hal, "Allan, Saskatchewan. My father voted for you!"

The old Chief's eyes got a little dreamy. "Ahh, yes, yes; the Anthony family. Wonderful family, wonderful. How is your father? How is Mr. Anthony?" "My father died some time ago Mr. Diefenbaker." "Sorry to hear that, and your mother, Mrs. Anthony?" "Dead as well, I am afraid." "Oh, I am sorry to hear that. The Anthony family. A wonderful family. Wonderful. I knew your parents well. The Anthonys, wonderful people. The whole Anthony family—wonderful." He signed the book and Hal moved on.

As Hal told the story, he would roll his eyes and say, "I didn't have the heart to tell the old bugger our family name is Bitz!" Hal may have used the name Hal Anthony on the air, but his real name was Harold Anthony Bitz.

It was several years later that Diefenbaker and I made up, at least sufficiently for him to agree to appear on our Christmas Cheer broadcast with me. Actually, he was delightful that day, witty, perceptive, dare I say even charming. We somehow got talking on-air about baseball, and Dief told a story which I have never forgotten:

"We had a pretty good baseball team back in Prince Albert when I was a kid," he says. "We didn't have much money, so in order to watch the game I would peak through a knothole in the wooden fence that surrounded the ballpark. One day as I had my eye glued to the hole, old Tom Ferguson, the local constable, booted me right in the behind so hard he almost drove me through the fence."

Ever the great public speaker, here Dief pauses for effect, then chuckles. "You know if I was driven through that fence and someone asked me how I got in, I would have replied, 'I was assed in!'"

· · ·

Bob

A few weeks later, in one of the bitterest leadership battles in Canadian history, Diefenbaker was defeated as leader of the Progressive Conservative Party by former Nova Scotia Premier Robert Stanfield. We can only speculate as to whether Diefenbaker would have had better success in three subsequent elections against the Pierre Trudeau-led Liberals. I am one of the few people in the country who believes that "The Chief" would have done better than Stanfield, one of the most surprisingly disappointing men I have ever interviewed.

Those who knew Stanfield well claim he was a kind and decent man, and I am certain he was, but if what I saw during the two hours he spent on my show was any indication, he would have made a terribly weak and indecisive leader of a country. I was astonished at his inability to answer the most simple of questions without first seeking advice from several "advisors" who joined him in the CFRA studio.

It was one of the most frustrating experiences of my career. A caller or I would ask Stanfield a question, and rather than responding immediately, he would cover the microphone with his hand and turn to one of his aides with an inquiring look. They would whisper something to him, at which point he would remove his hand from the "mike" and give us an answer, or more frequently what passed as an answer. I never saw a more indecisive man who would be leader in my life!

. . .

The Wise Guy

Your history books will tell you that three wise men came out of Quebec in the mid 1960s and more or less saved Quebec and Canada. Saved us from what, I am not exactly sure, since the threat of Quebec separation only got worse after the three arrived in Ottawa. Then, of course, we had the terrible scourge of FLQ terrorism, bombing, kidnappings and murder when one of the three wise men—Pierre Elliot Trudeau—was Prime Minister. I have no idea how wise the other two—Gerard Pelletier and Jean Marchand—were, but I do know that Jean Marchand was the cheapest little pipsqueak I have ever met.

He wanders into our little pet shop on Sparks street not long after he comes to Ottawa as a member of Parliament in 1965, complaining that the movers have broken the air pump on his aquarium filter. "Do I really need a filter," he asks, "or will the fish survive without one?" I assure him that without a filter all his tropical fish will surely die. "How much does a new pump cost?" he asks. After determining the size of his aquarium, I point out a dandy new filter that will do the job just fine for $6.95. This seems to stun him. "Does that include sales tax?" After some negotiation, I agreed to forgo the tax and ring up the sale.

A few days later, he is back with the pump. "I found a cheaper one," he explains. "I'd like my money back." I realize this guy is one big hotshot MP, acclaimed as one of the three wise men from Quebec and a good friend of Pierre Trudeau, so I am determined to keep my cool. After a bit of questioning, I learn that he, indeed, has found a cheaper air pump. He'd paid $5.95 for a smaller pump that I didn't think would do the job for him. I try to explain this without success, and reluctantly return his $6.95.

Several weeks later, he is back again, this time with the small pump. "I guess you were right," he says. "This pump isn't keeping my tank clean, I'll have to get that bigger one you sold me last month." My gloating comes to an abrupt halt when this wise guy goes to pay. "That will be $6.95—plus tax," I say. Marchand blinks. "You said I didn't have to pay tax." By this time I am starting to get a little hot under the collar, but once again I reluctantly agree to forgo the tax. Then guess what? Instead of handing me $6.95, he forks over the cheap little pump and a dollar! He wants me to accept his used pump and a buck as payment! I am sorely tempted to jump across the counter and grab the little weasel by the throat, but in the interests of national unity and hands across the border and all that stuff, I choke it all back and accept the deal.

As he walks out, I turn to a customer who has been watching all of this with astonishment and say, "If that's one of the three wisest men in Quebec, this country is in far greater trouble than anyone knows!"

· · ·

The Father of Medicare

The nicest politician I ever interviewed has to be Tommy Douglas, the man generally acknowledged as the father of Medicare in Canada. I had just started with CFRA and was sent to cover a giant farmer's rally on Parliament Hill.

It was the first time I had ever been on the Hill and one of the first live broadcasts I had ever done. I was intimidated and tremendously nervous. Tommy Douglas, leader of the newly formed New Democratic Party, sensed this and did everything in his power to assist in my interview with him, subtly suggesting a number of questions.

At one point we had to break away for news and I'll never forget Tommy sitting down on the front steps in front of the Peace Tower patiently waiting.

• • •

Ambassador Livingston, I Presume!

Almost as kind to me was the American Ambassador to Canada who arrived in the Capital the same week as I.

As any good journalist should, I have done my homework and have several, what I believe to be penetrating, questions concerning Canada-US relations.

"Ambassador Livingston," I ask, "what is your position on opening your borders to more trade?" I get a very reasoned response, although I get the impression he's looking strangely at me. I go through a list of other questions, always referring to him, as instructed, as Mr. Ambassador or Ambassador Livingston.

I feel pretty proud of myself when it's over. The rookie has done well, I tell myself.

As I am about to leave, the Ambassador quietly pulls me aside. "Mr. Green," he says, "I think you should know that my name is Livingston Merchant, not Merchant Livingston."

And you think *you've* been publicly embarrassed!

• • •

Kathleen

I know my career at CFRA is over when I walk into Kathleen Ryan's office and there, grim-faced, sits the Minister of Public Works for Canada, the Honourable George McIlraith.

It is Frank Ryan's office, but Frank is long since dead. His wife Kathleen now occupies the chair behind the huge desk. The black and white Holstein cowhide that adorned the front of his desk is still there, looking totally out of place, but then as far as I am concerned so does Kathleen.

I have a very good idea why I have been summoned to the office, but the presence of the Minister of Public Works is both puzzling and foreboding. No one bothers with introductions. "I gather this is about the Metcalfe Telephone System," I say. They both just look at me.

For the past several days, I have been waging a campaign to get a local company called the Metcalfe Telephone Company to provide proper service to its customers. A petition with several thousand names had been presented to me, outlining the incredibly primitive condition of the phone lines, some of which, believe it or not, were strung along fence posts. This, mind you, in a suburb of the Capital of Canada on the eve of our centennial celebrations.

I had gone out myself to have a look at the system and couldn't believe it. It was one of only a very few small independent phone companies left in the country, and I was publicly calling on the Federal Government to either compel the company to provide proper service or, barring that, force a sale to the Bell Telephone Company.

The residents of the Metcalfe area had come to me only after the Federal Government had thus far resisted all entreaties. Now I knew why. With the ghost of Frank Ryan rattling around in that second floor office, I have some facts of life explained to me.

The Minister of Public Works for the Government of Canada, one of the most influential and powerful men in Canada, George McIlraith is a major shareholder in the Metcalfe Telephone Company. I am after a tiger with a popgun! Is my goose cooked or what?

It is made very plain to me that it would be in the best interests of all concerned if I publicly apologize for my remarks about the Metcalfe phone service and withdraw my demand for Federal intervention.

My decision isn't difficult. Tiger, be damned. I'm not retracting a thing. In the best of Hollywood traditions, I inform them they can't fire me because I quit. This is a very stupid thing to do since it disqualifies me for a number of goodies, including unemployment insurance, and I must forfeit shares that Frank Ryan had given me in the station.

Pride is a wonderful thing but only when you don't let it get in the way of common sense. No matter. I walk out of the office, down the stairs and out onto Isabella Street, knowing I have done the only thing I can, but more than a little worried, no, make that scared.

It was like a bombshell had gone off in the city. First hundreds, then thousands of letters, petitions and phone calls of protest flood into the station and, as I learn later, into the offices of the Public

Works Minister of Canada and that of Prime Minister Lester Pearson. Plans are launched for a giant protest march on the station.

I am totally unaware of all of this, and am scrubbing the floor in our Sparks Street pet shop when I get the call. For the life of me, I cannot recall who it was on the phone, although I know it wasn't Kathleen Ryan. But I certainly remember the message: "Lowell, we'd like to have you back at CFRA. How soon could you return?" I have to get this straight. "No apologies, no retraction of the Metcalfe Telephone story?" "Absolutely not," is the reply. Next day I am back at work as though nothing had happened. The letters and petitions stop. The Metcalfe Telephone Company is sold to the Bell Telephone Company, telephone lines are strung onto telephone poles, telephones work as telephones should, and I don't lose a day of pay.

$$\bullet \ \bullet \ \bullet$$

On only one other occasion did Kathleen Ryan question me about anything. This time it wasn't an office command performance but a phone call at my desk. "Lowell, it's Kathleen Ryan here." I know who it is. You could not mistake her voice. "Lowell, why do you let," here she spit out the words, 'that woman' on the air?" I know exactly who she means. "That woman" is Charlotte Whitton, former Ottawa Mayor and now a City Councillor.

Several times a month I would get a call on the air from Charlotte which usually followed the same format. In her high-pitched voice, she would say something like: "Ahh, Green. As usual you do not have the faintest idea, no idea whatsoever what you are talking about." Then bang! Down would go the receiver as she hung up. It was great entertainment, since everyone in the city knew exactly who was calling.

"Mrs. Ryan," I reply, "that woman is the former Mayor of Ottawa and your sister!"

She harrumphs a couple times, but that is the end of the complaint.

Believe me, there was no sisterly love lost between Charlotte Whitton and her sister Kathleen Whitton Ryan.

Incredibly enough, years later when I decided to run in a provincial by-election in Ottawa Centre for the Liberals, George McIlraith delivers a ringing endorsement of my candidacy at the nomination convention. It is, indeed, a strange world sometimes.

• • •

Knudson

NOW ON THE FIRST TEE…LOWELL GREEN AND GEORGE KNUDSON, booms the public address system. I know it's rude to say this, but it is true: far from being scared stiff, I am so frightened the cheeks of my buttocks start to quiver.

I had only recently taken up golf. George Knudson was, until Mike Weir came along, the best male golfer this country had ever produced. Acknowledged as one of the greatest ball strikers in the game, George had represented Canada in nine World Cups, winning individual honours in 1966, and had won eight events on the PGA Tour.

Playing with him in the Pro Am tournament at the 1977 Canada Cup wasn't my idea. Come to think of it, I'm not sure whose idea it was, but there I am, teeing off in front of hundreds with one of the best golfers in the world. I am scared out of my wits. Don't laugh; you would be, too.

Hitting a golf ball reasonably straight is one of the most difficult tasks mankind ever invented for itself; doing it under circumstances such as this is just ridiculous.

George can see how pale I have become, and no doubt detects the quivering butt, so as I stride up to the first tee, he sidles up to me and says, *sotto voce*, "Remember, you'll still be alive tomorrow!" My laughter relieves the tension somewhat but not enough to stop me from slicing the ball well off to the right. Oh well, at least I don't whiff.

George doesn't say much else during the game, most of which is a blur to me until the very last hole. Anyone who has ever played the Hylands Golf Course out there near the MacDonald-Cartier Airport knows that the 18th hole is one of the toughest. The green is up against the clubhouse, guarded by a large pond, a pond that has destroyed the souls of more than a few golfers.

George hits one of his patented drives 280 or so yards straight down the middle, about 20 yards short of the pond, about 140 yards to the dreaded green. I get lucky and land my ball a few feet in front of George's. The only difference is it has taken me three shots to get there.

The word has spread that Green and Knudson are coming home (actually it is Knudson they want to see, they could have cared less about Green). A huge crowd has gathered around the 18th green and jams the balconies of the clubhouse. None of this bothers George. He lines up his shot and drops the ball about six feet from the hole. Loud and prolonged applause from the crowd!

I start to shake again. George stands there watching. The crowd stands there watching. The pond looms larger and larger. The green grows smaller by the moment.

Do I put it in the pond? Do I skull one and rap it off the clubhouse? Do I shank it off into the adjoining pasture? None of that.

Let the record show that I drop my ball at least two feet inside that of George Knudson's and almost faint! George stares at me a moment, starts to laugh, then says. "You've been holding out on me!"

Amazingly enough, some seven years later, I meet George coming off the Lucayan Golf Course in Freeport, Grand Bahama Island. He is dying of cancer at the time and I suspect is being treated at a well-known cancer treatment centre on the Island. He recognizes me immediately. "How's your game coming?" he asks. "A bit better than when I played you," I say, grinning. "Geez," he says, "are you giving lessons? I could use one!" We both laugh and go our separate ways.

He died shortly after.

. . .

That Dear, Sweet Soot Face!

As wives are wont to do from time to time, mine asked me the other day when I first knew I was in love with her. "Ahh," said I. "When first I saw that dear, sweet soot face!" At which we both burst out laughing. But it's true. It was, indeed, that dear, sweet soot-covered face that launched love.

The clarity that descends with approaching old age and the long distance of time has convinced me I was a little crazy when I met Deborah. I am certain she will be the first to agree, and just as quick to claim credit for rescuing me from the foggy whirlwind into which I had submersed myself. I'd better explain.

When Kitty and I married in 1961 we were, as Grandpa Green used to say, "babes in the woods." She from Moncton, New Brunswick, I from small-town Ontario, so naive, some would say dumb, we once carted home an empty Mateus wine bottle as a souvenir of our first-ever holiday. And like many young couples of the day, we had no money to speak of.

I have tried to convince the beautiful woman who is my first-born, Danielle, that her love of the outdoors today is a direct consequence of spending the first six months of her life in a tiny unheated cottage near Aylmer, Quebec, without running water or indoor plumbing. She, giggling with baby delight during diaper changes beneath the shade of lovely spruce trees whose wind-tossed branches would sometimes gently sweep down to caress her tiny body.

Some 18 years later, however, when Kitty and I divorced, we had amassed a small fortune.

We were the perfect business team, if not the perfect married couple. I was the quintessential entrepreneur, opening businesses, buying property, writing and broadcasting. Kitty was the careful record keeper who kept it all running. We both worked incredibly hard. When the phone rang to announce the birth of our second daughter, Lianne, I was on my hands and knees scrubbing the floor of our tiny pet shop at 250 Sparks Street. When we moved to our first home in Point Gatineau, Danielle and Lianne each morning had their mischievous, lovely little blond heads parked at the babysitters while I, in our ancient Renault, headed for CFRA on Isabella Street and Kitty hitchhiked to her job in Hull.

The first few years of The Little Farm Pet Shop provided far more laughs and tears than it did money. I remember closing up one Saturday at 9 p.m. with only 12 dollars in the till. "Imagine that," I said to Kitty, "12 hours, 12 dollars!" She was invited to some kind of day camp one Saturday and returned with exciting news. She had sold two hamster cages.

It was probably the bear cubs that turned it around for us. We were running a boarding kennel near Wakefield by this time and had a neighbour who had somehow acquired a pair of bear cubs. I thought they might create a bit of excitement around Sparks Street, so we loaded them into the back seat of our old Ford one day and took them to town for a bit of an adventure. When it became obvious they were going to rip our tiny pet shop to shreds in no time flat, Kitty decided to take them for a little hike.

The sight of a beautiful woman strolling along Sparks and Wellington Streets with two frolicking bear cubs in tow created no small sensation. And when the cubs darted up a tree on the front lawn of the Supreme Court and refused to come down, the news spread so fast the Parliament Buildings were soon emptied and Wellington Street completely blocked with the curious and, in some cases, the furious.

Business picked up dramatically after the front-page pictures in the *Citizen*!

Probably out of spite, the federal government shortly after that expropriated our little pet shop to build that monstrosity called 240 Sparks. In fact, the next time you're in that building, would you mind looking around for our missing monkey?

George the Spider Monkey was a major attraction with us for about a year. Reasonably well-behaved and polite, he fell in love with Elmer Diefenbaker, who often ended his daily wanderings with a visit to our pet shop before heading back to Stornoway. Elmer, either by design or accident, released George from his cage one day. George, recognizing a kindred spirit, immediately sprang onto Elmer's shoulder chattering happily away and thus began an almost daily routine for several months. George bouncing and gibbering on Elmer's shoulder as they meandered around the store, customers often poking each other in the ribs, pointing and whispering—"that's John Diefenbaker's brother!" More than one cynic was heard to ask, "Which one is the brother?"

There was a brief George and Elmer separation when the owner of the billiard parlor next door insisted we sell George to him so he could be taught to play pool. I tried dissuasion, pointing out that it was impossible to toilet train any monkey. That was bad enough, but George immediately developed a craving for blue chalk which, in addition to depleting the supplies, created a colourful rainbow residual without in any way improving the bouquet.

The monkey and the former prime minister's brother were soon reunited while the billiard parlour was fumigated, but one day George mysteriously disappeared. One moment he was there in his cage, the next moment he was gone without a sound or trace. Elmer was heartbroken and a few days later he just stopped coming. We never saw him again.

Some occupants of 240 Sparks today complain of strange sounds in the ceiling and sometimes catch brief glimpses of something darting around corners. I suspect it's George's ghost, or maybe Elmer's!

Now that I can laugh about it, I've often compared myself to George. One minute I'm there in that wonderful, wandering old house on Carmen Road near Wakefield with my wife, my daughters, two horses, a dog and a ton of money, the next minute I am holed up in the Algonquin Apartment Hotel on Cooper Street, with a few stray bits of refugee furniture for company.

I don't know about George, but I was heartbroken. Devastated. Angry and confused. Most of all overwhelmed by a sense of sadness in having failed my children. By this time, Danielle was pretty well on her own, living in residence at Sir John Abbot CJEP on the grounds of my old alma mater at MacDonald College in Ste Anne de Bellevue. Lianne was still at home, and while neither of them ever expressed it outright, I could sense their hurt. As a little boy, I had promised myself I would never do to my children what had happened to me.

I obviously should not have worried so much. My daughters today are marvelously unscarred by it all. Danielle has a really tough life spent hiking between one of Virginia's finest homes and a regal yacht in the Bahamas. That's when she and her husband Rob aren't exploring the Amazon or tooling up and down French canals in houseboats.

Lianne is one of the happiest people I've ever met and has brought us all much joy by presenting us with what is undoubtedly the cutest, smartest, sunniest little granddaughter on the face of the planet. A granddaughter who has done much to help heal old wounds and bring families together. The little guy with the big brown eyes, our grandson Peyton, has helped bring us together, as well. When Deborah's daughter Danya and her husband James decided to start a family, they returned from Vancouver to Ottawa in order to be close to us. Grandchildren are wonderful in more ways than one!

Ken "The General" Grant once suggested Kitty deserved the Order of Canada for staying married to me for 19 years. Maybe so. Maybe so. If that is the case, surely Deborah deserves sainthood for not only living with me for almost 25 years, but agreeing, as my current wife, to attend family functions attended by my former wife. Life is just too darn short to carry grudges, besides which Kitty and I get along better today than we ever did when married! Some may think it strange, but I can tell you our children and grandchildren love the fact that we get together for things like Christmas and birthdays.

As we all gathered at the dinner table last Christmas—great-grandmother Ella (aged 92), grandparents, parents, children and grandchildren—Lianne, who's not crazy about turkey, turned to me and said, "Dad, you have no idea how great it is not to have to eat two of these this year!"

A far cry, indeed, from the travel-industry Christmas party in 1980 where I first met Deborah.

I'd been single for about a year. She for several months. Her marriage breakup was one of those modern, civilized affairs; mine had been anything but and had left me terribly shaken. I had retired from CFRA and "The Greenline" to launch Ottawa Travel with three partners in 1978. We acquired Algonquin Travel about the day Kitty and I split, and interest rates had soared to about 20 percent which virtually doubled our loan payments. The banks were threatening to call our loan and put us out of business. Life wasn't a whole lot of fun! The only good thing about it was I lost more than 20 pounds. The problem was I was now so broke I couldn't afford to have a tailor take in the seat of my pants! Most mornings I didn't want to get out of bed.

Some men find escape in booze. I chased women and actually caught a few, including a beautiful blond but whacko New York doctor who tried to lure me to the Big Apple, then threatened to have me shot when I refused! (This was before "The Sopranos"!)

I was actually chasing another blond when I spotted a pair of gorgeous dancing legs topped by the most interesting and beautiful brown eyes I had ever seen. Forget the blond!

Courting Deborah wasn't easy. To be perfectly honest, she scared the heck out of me. So totally a feminist (only slightly radical) that on our first date I had to ask her if she minded if I opened the car door for her. I'll never forget her response: "Not if you don't mind if I open the door for you!" What was I getting into here?

Actually I was convinced our first date was a total bust. I pulled out all the stops. Took her to the finest restaurant in town, ordered the best wine, hit her with all my best jokes. Barely a chuckle. The most serious little face I'd ever seen. I feared disaster.

As I drove her home that night I figured that was the end of that when she suddenly turned to me and said, "I have a confession to make." "Oh, oh," I said to myself, "here it comes. Bye, bye, Charlie!" I concentrated on the steering wheel. "What's that?" She turned to me. "I don't have a very good sense of humour," she said.

I burst out laughing. "Thank God!" I said. "I thought I was striking out."

The next day came a knock on my door and there she was with two little kids in tow. While she didn't say it in so many words, the message was clear. If you're interested in me, this is what I come with; here's the whole package.

Danya had just turned seven, as cute as a button with her two pigtails, but Jeremy who was approaching five was a somewhat different kettle of fish. He was mostly nose and legs, neither of which ever seemed to stop running. Worse, he had a McDonald's addiction. "Pleased to meet you, Mr. Green," said Danya, obviously well-coached. "I want to go to McDonald's," said Jeremy swiping his nose with his sleeve and dashing up the corridor. Deborah looked a bit sheepish. "Jeremy loves McDonald's," she explained. Which turned out to be the understatement of the year!

My life at the time was in total chaos. Still reeling from the divorce, fighting off the banks, starting a new talk show with CKOY, crazy relationships. In Deborah I sensed an anchor, a firm hand to haul the flailing kite out of the windstorm. But she was totally different from any woman I had ever met before. Intelligent, serious, honest almost to a fault, completely incapable of deceit…but most of all from a different generation. She was 12 years younger than I. Could this really work?

The soot face decided it!

I dropped in to see her one morning about a month after that first date. She had moved in with a girlfriend who owned an old house in Centretown.

The front door was open. No one seemed home. I called Deborah's name a couple of times with no response, then noticed something very strange. The entire house was covered in black, oily soot. It coated the furniture, the walls, the carpet, the counters, even the ceiling. An obvious furnace intestinal eruption! Alarmed, I ran upstairs and there she was. Deep in the sleep of the innocent. Startling! Hilarious! If you saw Al Jolson in *The Jazz Singer*, then you get a pretty good idea what that face looked like: black as a crow's belly, save for a thin strip of pink along the upper lip marking the route of an exploring tongue.

My laughter woke her with a start—dark brown eyes in circles of white, stark against the black of her face and hair. Deborah, never particularly sunny or alert before morning coffee, was not amused by my laughter. "What's so funny?" she demanded, having not yet noticed the blackened sheets and blankets. I retrieved a small mirror from the bathroom and held it up. "Here! Whose funny little face is this?" "Oh, my God!" she shrieked and hurled the mirror away like some hideous bug. We looked at each other and the laughter started. Laughter until the tears rolled down both our cheeks, each drop of hers tracing a tiny path of pink through the black of her face, straight into my heart.

"You know what?" I said when I finally caught my breath. "I think you had better move that dear, sweet soot face in with me."

And that's where it's been ever since.

• • •

July 1, 1995. Deborah finally makes an honest man of me.

Oh, happy day! Deborah gets her Master's degree and can now start supporting me. Left to right: Jeremy, Deborah, Danya, a friend and my sister-in-law Mary Helen.

My second-born, Lianne, with my two grandchildren at last year's Help Santa Claus Parade. I founded this parade, the first of its kind where Santa is presented with gifts for less fortunate children. It was one of the most difficult tasks of my life, compounded by a very angry Joe Brown and the Happy Wanderers Band. Unprepared for the avalanche of gifts, we filled a truck and then dumped everything through a window into the ground floor studio of CFRA on Isabella Street. With several feet of toys blocking the door, the Happy Wanderers the next day had to scramble through a window with their equipment to get into the studio for their radio broadcast and then clear a path to the microphones. Joe Brown threatened to kill me, then had a great laugh. The firefighters have taken the event over and do a great job.

Danielle and Rob tie the knot on a tiny beach in the Bahamas.
My first-born has now become a Yank!

The Herald

Almost as scary as playing golf with George Knudson is carrying shopping bags filled with $13,000 in small bills halfway across Ottawa in broad daylight.

The *Sunday Herald* newspaper, which I had started on a shoestring in March of 1983, won the contract to publish and sell special souvenir booklets commemorating the papal visit to Ottawa in 1984. We had expected to make a fortune, which the cash-starved *Herald* could certainly have used, but for reasons we could never figure out (maybe because I'm Protestant!), sales had been very poor. Instead of the $100,000 we had expected to collect, the grand total came to just over $13,000, all of which had been delivered by Brink's to the Bank of Montreal on Sparks Street.

Not interested in running up another bill with Brink's, Deborah and I decide we can transport those few measly dollars in our pockets back to the *Herald*. Since you can't drive on Sparks Street, and parking within half a dozen blocks of the place costs a small fortune, we decide to walk from our Catherine Street office, a distance of at least 20 blocks.

A very serious dilemma presents itself immediately upon arrival. All the money is in small bills. We can't believe the huge pile of ones, twos, fives and tens that confronts us. The next problem is what to carry the money in. I had assumed the bank would have some special bags or carrying cases for us, but the manager looks at me like I am crazy when I tell him we are walking and don't even have a shopping bag.

A clerk finally takes pity on us and rounds up two Eaton's shopping bags which we jam full. With beating hearts, we head out onto the street, expecting at any moment to be mugged or worse.

This isn't just one of the first *Ottawa Sunday Herald*, this is the original *Herald*—the first copy of the first run of the city's first Sunday newspaper—now the *Ottawa Sun*.

In retrospect, there probably wasn't a crook in the world who would even dream that a couple strolling along clutching two shopping bags would be so stupid as to have them jammed with money. We make it back to the *Herald* safely, but it is one of the longest strolls I have ever taken.

The only other time I ever saw this much money piled in one spot was the day two "Valley lads" march into our office, one of them in rubber boots, and dump $20,000 on my desk.

Experts told me I needed at least a million dollars to start a newspaper, even one published only on Sundays. I managed to round up only $100,000, so almost from day one we were in desperate need of money. I didn't hide this fact from my employees in hopes they would moderate their agitation to form a union and postpone demands for higher wages at least until we really got going.

After a particularly hectic day during which my editorial staff decided to start a feud with production (they built a wall of beer cases between the two departments!), one of my sportswriters slips into my office and closes the door behind him.

"Need some money?" he asks. I don't tell him it is a silly question even though it is, so I just kind of nod. "How much?" "As much as we can get." He looks at me for a moment. "Are you pretty sure you can pay it back?"

My brain kicks into gear. "Wait a minute. What are we talking about here? What kind of interest are we talking about? What are the conditions? I'm not getting into bed with anyone who deals in lead pipes."

He's very indignant. "No interest," he says. "No lead pipes. What do you think I am anyway? These are good guys, they just want to help."

As I suspected, what he was talking about was a couple "good ole boys" from up the Valley who provided a bit of a service to a few people who liked to place a few bets from time to time. Nothing to do with drugs or theft or anything nasty. Personally, I have always believed that if I want to gamble a bit on the ponies or a football team with the little trickle of money governments leave me after taxes, that's my business. I am not in the least ashamed to say I accepted their "help."

The next day two guys, honest-to-goodness, one of them in rubber boots, walk into my office and without saying a word dump the contents of two gym bags onto my desk. There it is—$20,000 in small bills. I don't sign a thing. They don't say a word. Just take their empty bags and leave.

It is a fact that I have never before revealed: the *Ottawa Sunday Herald*, which is now the *Ottawa Sun*, was saved, not by the banks which wouldn't touch us with a ten-foot pole but by two bookies looking for a safe place to hide a bit of money!

Today, of course, the biggest bookie in the country is the government, so it's all legal. The only difference is there's no way the government would ever dump a dollar on my desk, let alone $20,000.

This, they tell me, is real progress.

Many of our financial troubles occurred as the result of a truly incredible decision by the printers union at *Le Droit* newspaper. One of the first things I did when deciding to launch a Sunday newspaper was line up a printer. I struck a deal with *Le Droit* to handle all of our print work, with the first payment not due until 30 days after our first edition to give us time to get some cash rolling in from advertisers.

Less than a week before our launch, the union, incredibly, voted not to accept the job. They didn't want the extra work! I had to scramble around and find a printer in Quebec at the last minute that demanded vastly different terms than those agreed to by *Le Droit*. This threw our entire cash-flow projections into the wastebasket. To complicate matters even further, a major advertiser who had committed to a full two-page spread in our centre section for the first four editions backed out only 24 hours prior to our launch.

The joys of doing business in Canada!

One of the biggest mistakes I made when recruiting investors for the *Herald* was selling a few shares to a local "psychic" who for fear of a lawsuit I will simply call "Ernie." This guy, within a few weeks, apparently was talking to some "spirits" who informed him that he should take over the reins of the paper. To accomplish this, he decided to cause as much trouble for me as possible by feeding stories, some true, some not so true, to the *Ottawa Citizen* which eagerly devoured reports about employee dissension, shortage of money, and so on, all fed to them by our fortune-telling friend.

In an effort to shut this bird up, the Board of Directors agreed to buy him out and called a meeting to negotiate the purchase. Earl Montagano, co-owner of the Ottawa 67's at the time, was renting us the basement of a building he owned on Wellington Street and offered the use of his third-floor boardroom.

During the meeting, Board member Kenny Lehman, a former Ottawa Rough Rider star lineman, became very agitated with "Ernie," accusing him of stabbing us in the back. The meeting grew hotter and hotter until, without warning, another one of our Board members, Chuck Brown of Chuck Brown Golf, suddenly reached across the table and grabbed the smirking snitch by the throat. "You little ##**##**," he roared, "I'm going to drop you out the window." His wife, Ottawa City Councillor Jill Brown, shouted, "Chuck, Chuck, we're on the third floor." "Alright then," says Chuck, "we'll move to the sixth floor!"

It was at about that point that our boy "Ernie" decided to sell.

Despite all of this, and a great deal more, we somehow managed to survive, sometimes forestalling the bank by only a few hours. I sold out to partners and they, in turn, sold to the *Sun*, finally creating what I firmly believed Ottawa desperately needed: a second daily newspaper.

· · ·

Rich

I've sold the *Herald*. I haven't taken a major business risk in at least a couple of weeks, so what the heck, let's start a radio station!

Actually the idea is that of Gord Atkinson, a pioneer broadcaster in Toronto and Ottawa. He's retired as general manager of CFMO-FM in Ottawa (now Bob-FM) and gets a brilliant idea. The local CBC station is shutting down its AM operation and instead will operate two FM stations. (What the heck, it's taxpayers' money, right?) This means not only is there a vacant AM frequency available in Ottawa, but also a fully operational AM transmitter.

He contacts his lifelong friend Rich Little, in Hollywood, who agrees to finance the deal. I do a business plan, line up some prospective employees, fill out reams of paperwork, and hire one of the best accountants in town, Rick Shorkey, who's also a good friend. After my experience trying to run a newspaper on a shoestring, I decide to line up a few more dollars and approach Rod Bryden, who of course later will save the Ottawa Senators. Rod is interested but wants to see the colour of Rich Little's money first. Fair enough.

Rich is financing all of this as we go along, including a deposit to the CBC to insure we get the right of first refusal for the transmitter site. Rich's "handlers" are getting a little antsy in light of Rich's impending divorce, so Gord decides to get Rich up here to have a look at what he's paying for.

The transmitter site is in the middle of a cow pasture in the southwest end of Ottawa. It boasts several of those spindly, tall towers with red lights on top that you see all over the place. Situated in the middle of the field is a small building jammed with tubes and wires and whirling things.

Rich tries to look interested in the tubes and wires, but I can see his eyes beginning to glaze over as Gord enthuses about wattage and broadcast signals and programming.

Rich stops. "What's that?" He points to a loonie someone has dropped on the floor. "A loonie," says Gord. "That's our new dollar. You haven't seen one?"

Now Rich is fascinated. He picks up the coin and turns it over, slowly examining the design on both sides. "That's a Canadian dollar?" He seems incredulous. "What happened to the paper dollar?" All interest in transmitter sites is now abandoned while Gord explains loonies and toonies. Rich demands to see a toonie and luckily I have one in my pocket. He turns this around, pokes at the middle trying to extract it, shakes his head and chuckles.

As we exit the building, several cows look up with hungry eyes and begin to moo gently. Rich is fascinated all over again. He walks over, talks to the cows, plucks a bit of grass and hands it to them through the fence. Finally we leave.

All of this convinces me that Rich Little doesn't have much interest in a radio station, but whether he does really makes no difference since shortly after this we are advised that Rich's divorce is much more expensive than anyone suspected and any major projects are now on hold.

Imagine that, an expensive divorce!

I think the transmitter site is still there and so is the frequency, but these days a new AM frequency is hardly worth a loonie, let alone a toonie!

. . .

The Party Guy

Tomorrow the fate of Canada will be decided; we will be conducting the most important broadcasts of our lives. But tonight Steve Madely wants to go to Gibbys!

We have spent most of the afternoon and evening setting up our remote broadcast location on Ste Catherine Street in the heart of Montreal. I am very worried about the referendum for separation that will be held tomorrow; I'm tired; I want to go back to our hotel and go to bed.

"Let's go to Gibbys," says Steve. I check my watch. "Steve, for God sakes, it's almost 9:00. You've got to be up at 4:30 tomorrow morning for your show. If they vote to separate tomorrow, all hell will likely break lose and we'll be in the middle of it. I'm dead tired, let's call it a day."

"Let's go to Gibbys," he says.

That's how we end up at one of Old Montreal's most famous steak houses at 10:00 p.m., October 29, 1995. It is fitting, I suppose. Gibbys is only a stone's throw from the Montreal City Hall balcony from which Charles de Gaulle shouted his infamous, "Vive le Quebec Libre."

By the time we leave Gibbys, it is referendum day. He wants to go uptown to see what's happening, but I do manage to talk him out of that.

The next morning starting at 6:00, with less that four hours sleep, Steve Madely conducts one of the best shows I have ever heard him do, in the bitter wind, the cold and the tension that was Ste Catherine Street, October 30, 1995. It was the day we came within one half of one percentage point of seeing Canada split apart.

My programs that day and the next were broadcast from downtown Montreal to Halifax, Montreal, Windsor, Sudbury and

Winnipeg, as well as Ottawa, the largest private radio network in Canadian history.

Don't think for a moment that Steve takes anything he does lightly. He does not. Steve Madely is the Mario Lemieux of broadcasting. He never appears to be working too hard, but gets the job done superbly, aided greatly by the happy faculty of being able to absorb tremendous amounts of information very quickly and haul it out of his brain when needed, perhaps years later.

Despite appearances to the contrary, he is always well-prepared. Prior to his morning broadcast from the Winnipeg flood of 1997, for example, he insists that we both spend half the night touring the city and adjoining St. Boniface to insure that we have good grasp of the overall situation. Within a few hours, Steve knows more about the flood than reporters who have been there from day one.

His finest hour, undoubtedly, was the key role he played in the October 27, 1995, giant rally in Montreal, which probably saved the country. It was Steve Madely who first proposed the rally and promoted it very heavily, but when the work is done and there's a Gibbys or party nearby, Steve will be there.

He is a genuinely nice guy, but I learned long ago there is no sense in me even trying to keep up with him. By the time I'm ready to leave for home, Madely is ready to leave for a place with more action. While covering the Winnipeg flood, we got stuck without a car in a small motel miles from downtown, and it almost drove him crazy that the best entertainment we could drum up was Red Lobster.

One thing that Steve Madely definitely is not is an athlete. Former CFRA general manager Terry Kielty can attest to that. We held our annual horseshoe party at Terry's summer cottage near Chaffey's Locks on the Rideau System until one of Madely's horse-

The fishermen return! Steve Madely, grinning ear to ear, caught a bucketful of fish with his $4.95 rod. Dave McLelland, decked out in his special rain gear, caught a tree branch!

shoes ended up dangling from the Kielty television aerial. On another occasion during a tournament at Hal and Gloria Anthony's home in Kemptville, Madely lost a shoe in a nearby tree. Both times, I assure you, he was dead sober

To golf with Steve Madely is very risky business. He is, however, perhaps the luckiest fisherman I have ever met. Debbie and I invited Steve and his wife Gale and another couple, Dave and Sharron McClelland, to our Lake Opinicon cottage for a weekend of fishing. Dave, who owns one of Ottawa's most successful advertising agencies, prides himself on being an expert fisherman and shows up with a most wonderful assortment of rods, reels and lures.

When I say rods, that's what I mean—at least four of them all stored in a large case that looks very much like the thing Al Capone used to lug his machine gun around in. Madly, not to be outdone, appears with one of those $4.95 Canadian Tire rods that telescopes down to a handful. The yellow plastic margarine container is a bit of a puzzle until Steve opens it to reveal two cheap metal lures that look fresh from Cracker Jack boxes. As you can imagine, there is great hilarity, with Dave assuring Steve that he will show him some real fishing and might even loan him a lure or two.

You know what happened, don't you? Right! It is pouring rain the next morning so I fake a headache or something, but there is no holding back those two. As you might expect, Dave has a complete professional head-to-toe slicker that probably set him back a few hundred dollars. Steve borrows an old sweater of mine.

When I set out several hours later to locate them in the dense fog that has settled over the lake, I track them down by the sound of Steve's laughter and Dave's swearing. *Flick* goes the $4.95 rod and the cheap lure. Bang! A bite and a nice big bass. *Swish* goes the $200 rod and the $20 lure. Nothing. All morning. Bang! on the $4.95! Nothing on the $200 jobbie!

Fortunately, we are well-stocked with Dave's favourite Scotch whiskey and by noon he has decided not to burn his slicker and his rods, although he does manage to fling several of his expensive lures into some heavy brush.

Steve shades his eyes, leans forward in the "explorer" attitude, peers in the direction of the hurled lures and says, "Way to go, Dave! You caught a branch!"

• • •

The Gomery Game

The most vivid memory I have of John Gomery is of him teaching me a pretty neat parlour game involving nine pieces of paper and a cane. The year was 1956. John was about to be called to the bar. I was in my final year at MacDonald College and was dating his sister Judy. We, of course, had no idea that one day John might help bring down a government.

For the life of me, I cannot recall who was there, other than John, Judy and I, but there was a living room full of people at the Gomery home in Montreal West waiting out a rainy Saturday afternoon. Things were dragging a bit when John announced that he was developing some psychic abilities and if anyone was willing to challenge him he could prove that he could actually read minds. There was a fair amount of derision.

"All right," he said, "Judy, give me a hand to find some sheets of paper," and they disappeared into the kitchen. They reappeared a few moments later with nine sheets of blank paper which they laid on the living room floor—three rows across the top, three rows in the middle, another three rows along the bottom—in other words three rows of three—this is important.

"Now," said John, "I'm going into the kitchen—Lowell you start—tell Judy which piece of paper you are thinking of and when I come out I will identify it. I chose the lower right-hand sheet. John then re-entered the room. Using a cane she had picked up as a pointer, Judy first tapped the upper right hand sheet. "Okay, John," she said, "if you're so smart, tell me which sheet of paper Lowell is thinking of. Is it this one?" John closed his eyes, in apparent deep contemplation. "No." "Is it this one?" she asked, pointing to the middle sheet. The same deep concentration. "No." She pointed to a couple more sheets, asking the same question each time. The reply was always the same. "No." Until, lo and behold, she pointed to the lower right hand sheet. "Is it this one?" John's eyes flew open. "Yes, yes, that's the one."

Loud applause and, naturally, a challenge from someone else. But it was always the same. John was able to identify the correct sheet each time. We suspected Judy was giving him some kind of verbal message, so we insisted she ask different questions. The result was the same. John was always able to identify the correct sheet of paper.

I harassed him until he finally explained the secret. I've played the game many times over the years. It's great fun and never fails to stump most people. These days when I tell them it's "the Gomery Game," they are mightily impressed.

What's the secret?

Well, if I tell you here, then everyone who reads this book is going to know which will pretty well destroy the mystery. So here's the deal. I will reveal the secret to anyone who asks me, in person, on the phone, by mail or email. Just say, Lowell what's the secret to the Gomery Game? And then only three people will know—you, me and the judge!

Judy Gomery, by the way, married one of my MacDonald classmates, Milt Hooker, who has the farm right next door to that of my brother Barry in Ormstown. Is it a small world or what? Barry raises world champion boxer show dogs in partnership with my daughter Lianne. Just thought I'd get that little plug in!

· · ·

The End and the Beginning

Each spring for many years, my father and his brothers and sisters and I revisited our childhoods and assembled for a day of chub fishing in the muddy little creek that ran along behind our Stumptown farm.

My father from his farm in Ormstown, Quebec, Cecil from St. Clair Shores in Michigan, Ken from Sundridge, Ontario, Nilah, Genevieve, Willard and Orlo from London. The creek, sometimes not much more than a trickle, is obviously polluted by the cows which often stand knee-deep in it, only a few hundred yards upstream. Often Niles, Genevieve's son from Lucan, who used to keep us supplied with mud turtles, joins us as well.

The chub, if any are ever caught, aren't much bigger than sardines and would probably give you any number of diseases if you dared eat them. But for those of us who grew up in that tiny farmhouse, shouting distance away, the creek and in particular the old stone railway arch that spans it are magic. This is where we all learned to swim and whiled away countless summer hours in sunny innocence so many years ago. This is where Ken first launched his homemade boat *Le Corbeau* and where we all laughed ourselves silly as it immediately began to sink with Virgil at the helm, water lapping his chest, shouting, "The captain always goes down with the ship."

I was at the old arch when I first became aware I loved my father. He had returned to Arthur for a brief leave from the army. The train all the way from Texas to Toronto. Hitchhiking all night from Toronto, then walking the final mile or so up the Stumptown Road, arriving just before dawn.

He awakens me by tossing stones against my bedroom window. I somehow manage to make it downstairs and out the door without disturbing the household, although I believe my grandparents are fully aware of what is happening.

My father picks me up and tosses me into the air.

"Come on, big boy, let's go see the sunrise."

And so we do, walking hand in hand along the railway tracks to the old arch. There we stand together, tossing pebbles into the water as the sun slowly creeps above the horizon.

I cannot today, more than 60 years later, see a sunrise without remembering that wonderful morning.

The old farmhouse has long since crumbled and disappeared. For a long time the cement silo stood solitary guard, but it too has now been bulldozed. The creek and the arch, now crumbling, still remain, but even the railway tracks, which during the war took so many fathers and brothers away and brought some of them home, are gone. Ripped up for progress.

The "Old Arch" where Lowell's father caught his last fish. The waters are muddy, but the memories are grand. My aunt Nilah has gone "modern" with that rod and reel.

The last time I went to our annual chub fishing reunion the weather was bitterly cold and we had to hunker down behind some bushes for protection from the wind. It didn't matter much, we were glad to see each other again, and in particular, to take up another family tradition: poking fun at my father's fishing pole.

The pole was something right out of Tom Sawyer—bamboo and a full 20 feet long. Several years before, it had been run over by one of my uncles, accidentally he claims. It had been patched with black tape and was perfectly functional.

We told the usual stories about getting the pole down from cousin Donalda's drive shed and manoeuvring it through the streets of Arthur lashed to the roof of our car. Cecil would have his usual supply of wonderful butter tarts, purchased at the local gas station.

My father and I fishing at the "Old Arch" just weeks before he died. Shortly after this picture was taken, my father caught his last fish—a giant shiner at least four inches long, the source of much brotherly and sisterly derision.

What I didn't know, but suspected, was that my father was dying. A form of leukemia had been diagnosed. By the time chub fishing time rolled around, the results of the disease were evident.

He was insistent, though, and so off to Arthur we drove. I helped him walk the few hundred yards up the railway bed, and there atop the old arch, he tossed in his hook and worm and caught a fish. A whopper, at least two inches long! The whoops and catcalls from his brothers and sisters were wonderful.

We talked about that fish, my father and I, only a few hours before he died. He got a good chuckle out of it, all over again.

• • •

A Final Thought

It is incredible to think that when my grandfather Henry Green was born in that little Stumptown house, Canada was only 15 years old. At the time, there wasn't a single automobile in all of North America, and Alexander Graham Bell had only just invented the telephone.

Henry Green was 11 when Wilber and Orville Wright introduced the world to manned flight at Kitty Hawk (December 17, 1903).

He was a young man of 17 when J.A.D. McCurdy took his famous flight in the Silver Dart at Baddeck, Nova Scotia (February 23, 1909). That was the first manned flight in the British Empire.

Yet before he died, men were walking on the moon!

When his mother (Mary Ann Gilder) was born, the age of steam and the Industrial Revolution had only just begun. Most of mankind could move no faster than a horse could draw or carry them. It had been that way since the dawn of civilization.

When she died, airplanes were ready to attack Europe and Britain at speeds well in excess of 300 miles per hour. Rockets were already on the drawing board. Radio broadcasts on one continent could be heard on another. Henry Ford was turning cars out at the rate of about one every hour.

In my lifetime, I have seen the birth of television, antibiotics, jet travel, space exploration and, of course, the computer. The advances in medicine have been astonishing.

Now consider this. Mary Ann Gilder was alive when I was born. Thus within the lifespan of only two people, we have gone from the speed of horses to Space Shuttle Columbia re-entering earth's atmosphere at 74,500 miles per hour! The sum of all the world's knowledge the day Mary Ann was born could today be stored in a microchip smaller than your hand.

We do truly live in an age of wonder!

But what we have seen since Mary Ann was born is nothing compared to what the children of my grandchildren will see. I don't want future generations reading this and poking fun at Grandpa Lowell's wild imagination, so I am not even going to attempt any predictions. Except to say that what lies ahead will be more astonishing than anything we have seen thus far.

Which one of my descendants, do you suppose, will be the first to set foot on another planet? What fun it would be if he or she added a chapter to this book.

• • •

New!

How the granola-crunching, tree-hugging, thug huggers are wrecking our country!

ISBN 978-1-894439-30-5   208 pages, hardcover
$32.95

In the unique style that has endeared him to one of Canada's largest and most loyal radio audiences, best-selling author Lowell Green launches an all-out exposé on those Canadians he says are wrecking our country. He tackles issues ranging from our dangerous refugee, immigration and multicultural policies to the soft-on-crime-gang with their needle and crack-pipe handouts, the Kyoto Accord, Canada's homeless "industry," and much more.

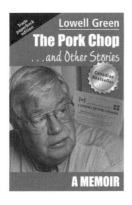

The Pork Chop...and Other Stories
A Memoir

ISBN 978-1-894439-32-9   256 pages, trade paperback
$24.95

To order copies of these books by Lowell Green,
contact Creative Bound Inc. at (613) 831-3641 (Ottawa)
or 1-800-287-8610 (toll-free in North America)

Ordering online is easy at **www.creativebound.com**

These books are also available at fine bookstores everywhere.